Act of Synod – Act of Folly?

Every part of the life of the Church, the totality of the system of communication by which it promotes its own coherence and effectiveness, ought to stand for a facet of the Gospel. There should not be a sharp division between what a Church teaches and how it manages its institutional arrangements . . .

Stephen Sykes, *Unashamed Anglicanism*

Act of Synod – Act of Folly?

Edited by
Monica Furlong

SCM PRESS

Introduction, Postscript and arrangement
copyright © Monica Furlong 1998
Chapters 1-7 copyright © individual contributors
1998

The quotation from Stephen Sykes, *Unashamed
Anglicanism*, published and © copyright 1995 by
Darton, Longman and Todd Ltd, is used by kind
permission of the publishers.

0 334 02746 2

First published 1998
by SCM Press
9-17 St Albans Place, London NI ONX

SCM Press is a division of SCM-Canterbury Press Ltd

Typeset by Regent Typesetting, London
and printed in Great Britain by
Biddles Ltd, Guildford and King's Lynn

Contents

Introduction

MONICA FURLONG

A few weeks ago a priest I know in the Southwark Diocese attended an ordination. At the rehearsal (she was to be the bishop's chaplain) she was approached by the Diocesan Director of Ordinands. 'You do realize that we have a problem with one of the candidates? He has requested that women do not lay hands on him – he has objected on grounds of authority.' Couched in terms of Christian charity and sweet reasonableness, this request that she must not touch the candidate was difficult to refuse, yet left a nasty taste behind it. My friend agreed, but says 'I was sickened by my own magnanimity.' The ordinand in question, an Evangelical, was, in his own way, making use of the 'doctrine of taint', pioneered by Forward in Faith, to put down a woman properly and legally ordained in the Church of England. Suppose, just suppose, that the DDO had said to the candidate, 'No, sorry, we value our women too much to discriminate against them in any way at all. Perhaps you have made a mistake in seeking ordination in the Church of England?' Suppose the moon is made of cream cheese. In the ethos set up by the Act of Synod the request seemed a perfectly natural one. That is why some of us oppose it.

In order to understand the Act of Synod 1993, it is necessary to set it in its historical context.

The original Measure to bring about women's ordination, which Synod voted for in November 1992, itself unashamedly supported discrimination. It said 'without prejudice to section

19 of the Sex Discrimination Act 1975, nothing in Part II of the Act shall render unlawful sex discrimination against a woman in respect of

(a) her ordination to the office of priest in the Church of England.

(b) the giving to her of a licence or permission to serve or officiate as such a priest;

(c) her appointment as dean, incumbent, priest-in-charge or team vicar . . .'

This daunting statement, it must be said, was agreed upon by the proponents of women's ordination (and defended, I think I am right in saying, by all the Anglicans who have contributed to this book, including myself, some of whom write here of their ambivalence about it). They, we, were between the devil and the deep blue sea. If we held out for a fairer form of legislation, the legislation itself would never reach Synod, and the hundreds of women waiting for ordination would remain frustrated. Bishop Peter Selby points out the oddness of the whole process 'in which those about whom the argument was raging had so little voice compared with those who opposed their ordination, and in which those who had made the implacability of their opposition clear still retained a strong voice in the detailed drafting of legislation they would in any case oppose'. He has written well of what he calls the 'tribalism' in the church which loses sight of it as an essentially 'adoptive' community.

In spite of the opponents the Measure went through with two-thirds majorities in all three Houses. This was no great surprise to some of us – though no previous Measure had ever achieved these voting figures – because thirty-three out of the forty-four dioceses had already indicated they were in favour. It did, however, appear to come as a surprise to both the bishops and to the opposition, as Peter Selby notes. The bishops had announced before the Measure that they would be 'keeping their diaries clear' in the week following it, assuming, it appears with hindsight, that they would be busy comforting unhappy women. The reality was rather different, and from all over the country women ordinands reported the shock of returning cheerfully to their dioceses, expecting joy and pleasure on their behalf, to find bishops and even vicars with faces as long as a boot. Jean Mayland reports the almost laughable mood of gloom and doom at Bishopthorpe in the York diocese. An article by the local bishop in *The Cornish Churchman* read: 'There is no point in mincing words, it is agony – agony for those who feel betrayed and mutilated by a Church they love.' The Bishop of Southwell compared the decision to bereavement, redundancy and divorce. As more than one woman noted, bishops in favour of women's ordination seemed little more enthusiastic than those against. Senior clergy who, often enough, had shown little interest in women's pain and frustration in the past, now seemed bent on forbidding them to be joyful, and worse, showed themselves unable even to be sympathetically happy on their account.

This would have been intolerable had not the laity, in many cases, shown enormous enthusiasm over what had happened. Women returned home to champagne, flowers, and rapturous messages. The Movement for the Ordination of Women office nearly broke down under the pressure of worldwide excitement. Nor, unusually, was the pleasure confined to churchgoers. A group of women and men, observing a three-day vigil outside Lambeth Palace which ended on the day of Synod's decision, found themselves hugely popular with passing motorists and lorry-drivers, some of whom brought them hot food and drink. As the vigil was reported on the *Today* programme the members of the vigil were affectionately hooted at and waved to by passing motorists listening in on their radios. In the evening after the vote a group of men and women, some of the women wearing dog collars, entered a pub in Westminster and received a standing ovation from the house. A group of businessmen meeting upstairs, sending down to find out what was going on, insisted on buying them all dinner. I was myself embraced lovingly in Dean's Yard by a Westminster schoolboy (completely unknown to me) and a journalist whom I had always regarded as entirely cynical on the issue. 'Vicars in knickers', the *Sun* enthused. For once the Church of England had touched a popular nerve. It appeared to give it little pleasure.

Instead all was concentrated on the rage of the defeated opposition. 'The conviction of two-thirds of churchgoing Anglicans was being set aside while all eyes were fixed on a vociferous minority,' wrote Margaret Webster. 'The women, who over so many years had been told that they must not speak about their pain and frustration, were now faced with the spectacle of the pain of the opponents being publicized with considerable effect.'[1] The Press spread themselves on this and blew the issue up into talk of breakdown and schism in the Church of England; church leaders, under tremendous pressure to 'do something' by the opponents of women's ordination, seemed to be suffering a collective *crise*. In January 1993 the bishops met in Manchester and produced what became known as 'the Manchester Statement'. Their primary concern continued to be with those who would not accept women priests, and inventing 'safeguards' to protect them. 'I find it offensive,' Tony Benn was later to remark in the House of Commons 'to be told that the House need not worry because there will be safeguards for male priests against ordained women coming into their parishes. Safeguards? My God! What sort of man wants a safeguard in case a woman gives communion in his parish?' The overriding interest of the meeting seemed to have been to keep the bishops united and avoid 'no go areas' i.e. dioceses in which bishops opted out altogether. No women, of course, were present at this meeting. From then on deals and concessions became the order of the day. Already, by February 1993, the bishops had conceded that they would continue to appoint bishops who were opposed to women's ordination, what they called 'non-discrimination in the choice of bishops'. 'Non-discrimination', the little Christian feminist scandalsheet *Uppity* sagely observed, 'means built-in discrimination against women.' *Uppity* also noted that such concessions did not for a moment placate those opposed, indeed Bishop Graham Leonard himself described the concessions, perhaps not without justice, as 'doctrinal levity'. 'All they have succeeded in doing is in making it clear that it is

tantrums which get attention and gain benefits', *Uppity* went
on. 'No sensible parent would run a family the way the bishops
are attempting to run the Church – in a good home one
learns quickly that drumming with one's heels doesn't pay.'[2]
Unfortunately in this case it did.

Cost of Conscience and the new organization to unite
opponents, Forward in Faith, continued to lobby strenuously,
and to organize mass meetings. It was suggested that many,
many priests would leave the Church of England, probably
somewhere between 1000 and 3000 (383 working priests
actually did so, 40 of whom returned.) This was worrying
because, as a result of the compensation measures written into
the legislation – around £30,000 for each priest who left – it
was going to cost the Church of England a great deal, this at a
time when it was reeling under the first shock of the financial
disaster of the Church Commissioners' investment policy. What
was much more striking than such practical worries, however,
was that the bishops collectively seemed to have an overwhelming sense of identification with the disaffected, and a feeling that
something must be done to relieve their distress. What seemed
baffling then, and seems baffling now, is their total inability to
identify also with the women and what they must be feeling as
their offering of themselves was debased with insulting concessions to those who opposed them. On the contrary, women
were, at times, given the feeling that the whole difficult situation
was their fault. It was assumed, alas, rightly, that the women
would go along quietly with the demeaning process of seeing the
provisions of the Measure substantially altered to their dis-
favour. Nothing perhaps could have better illustrated the male-
centredness of the Church of England, nor the difficulty church
women have in insisting on some sort of parity.

Jane Shaw has described the view of women, or rather two
overlapping views, that seems to her to inform the actions of
1992 and 1993, and to form the basis of both the original
legislation and the Act of Synod. One view of women is the
ancient hierarchical one, deeply embedded in our culture, that
woman somehow is *man*, but an inferior version of man. The

other view, popular since the Enlightenment, and used a good deal in the women's ordination debate, is of complementarity – the sexes are different but equal. The second theory, though at first sight more attractive, in practice, as she demonstrates, tends to confine women (and of course, men) to stereotypes which may be limiting and damaging. Speaking of the Measure and the Act of Synod she writes: It seems to me that older notions of gender hierarchy have melded with notions of sexual difference to create a fairly deadly mix in which women are simultaneously thought to be *both* the 'non-norm' . . . *and* different.' She goes on to show how this has opened the way to the archaic idea of 'taint'. 'The "theology of taint" which is a part of the reception (one might say ideological outworking) of the Act of Synod relies upon a notion of woman as utterly different, indeed untouchable. Here, woman may be equal in all other regards but her "difference" discards her into a space which makes her sacramental ministry literally – for some – polluting. In this view, once touched by hands which have laid hands on a woman, one is tainted.'

Such beliefs, not always fully conscious, informed the interior struggles in the church. Meanwhile, fresh problems arose as the whole issue began its passage through Parliament. This involved the setting up of an 'Ecclesiastical Committee' which began to meet in April 1993. It included, like the original committees in Synod, a generous sprinkling of those opposed root and branch to women priests. They were chosen, I believe I am right in saying, by asking for volunteers. Patrick Cormack MP was one member. He admitted to receiving hundreds of letters in favour, but nevertheless was firmly against the Measure on the grounds of 'expediency' and did, in fact, speak against it in the Commons debate. News kept leaking out about the hostility of the Committee to the whole project (another reason for women to keep quiet and not raise their heads above the parapet), and it was an astonishing surprise, therefore, when the debate in the House of Commons actually took place to find almost the entire House, Conservative, Liberal Democrat and Labour, not only technically 'in favour' but actually highly enthusiastic about women priests. Only a handful of MPs spoke against the Measure. The rumours of a hostile Parliament had been false.

However, the *fear* of the legislation falling down at the parliamentary fence had been very real. It lent a spurious authenticity to suggestions that the legislation, as it stood, was 'too liberal', 'did not make enough provision for those against' etc. The House of Bishops produced *Bonds of Peace*, the document for something quite new, The Act of Synod, which was to slew the whole emphasis of the Measure for Women's Ordination in a new direction, one more favourable to those opposed to women priests. With its echo of 'bondage', the title struck a rather ominous note to those of us more used to twentieth-century language than the tropes of St Paul. It was produced in June 1993, and briefly considered at the July Synod. It was only possible even to contemplate such an Act, of course, because the original Measure protected the church from the Sex Discrimination Act. The same devices, in a racial context, would have caused rioting and legal sanctions.

Judith Maltby and Jean Mayland, who laboured long and hard in Synod over the Measure itself, write of the haste with which this far-reaching bit of legislation was cobbled together, virtually without consultation outside the bishops' own ranks. They contrast this with the twenty years of so of debate at all levels which the Measure itself had received. The Act was applauded by the bishops themselves as a remarkable feat of episcopal collegiality, and we shall never know probably just how so much consensus was arrived at, with bishops who had hitherto been keen supporters of women priests apparently going along as meekly as lambs. The danger of collegiality, particularly if it is unexamined by outside and democratic influence, is obviously one of peer pressure. Only one bishop, John Baker of Salisbury, publicly uttered doubts. Judith Maltby suggests that the notion of collegiality may be 'borrowed clothes' (borrowed from the Roman Catholic Church), and that, within the very different context of a more democratic church, they may not fit so well or be entirely appropriate. In this case the borrowing virtually presented General Synod with a *fait accompli*. Peter Selby also has his doubts about collegiality, together with the concept of the bishop as a 'focus of unity'. Partly because of the Act of Synod he suggests that these ideas 'need much more questioning than they generally receive at times of severe controversy, times at which they could be as much temptation as resource'.

Bonds of Peace talked a great deal about generosity, compassion and the Anglican gift for compromise, and one has to read it with great alertness to see that the giving is all one way, from the women to those opposed to them. The giving meant that the original Measure, draconian as it was in its attitudes to women, was to be made much more severe. What became popularly known as 'the two integrities' i.e. that it was as legitimate to reject women priests as to accept them, was to mean that a kind of apartheid against women priests was to be officially sanctioned; although Synod and the dioceses had overwhelmingly chosen to have women priests, their clear choice was to be blurred. To assist in the task of 'separate development' three bishops, known as Provincial Episcopal Visitors, were to be consecrated, with a special remit for those opposed. The Act made it virtually impossible for women ever to become bishops, creating, as the monitoring organization WATCH (Women and the Church – the successor to MOW) puts it, 'a glass ceiling' which excludes women. Naughty *Uppity* printed 'Six Impossible Things about The Act of Synod to try to Believe Before Breakfast'. 'That it is about generosity and unity. That it is not about money. That it does not denigrate women. That it is a good example to the other churches. That it is not a wimpish solution. That it will lead to a happy outcome.'[3] The Act was, as Jean Mayland documents, in total denial of many fervent and apparently authoritative statements made by archbishops, bishops and influential Synod members in the past.

There were, of course, many within the Church of England who were profoundly unhappy with this turn of events, seeing it as an inability to face conflict. In October 1993, a few weeks before Synod was to vote on the Act, an Open Letter to the House of Bishops appeared in the *Church Times*.

We are very concerned that the Act of Synod proposed by the House of Bishops undermines the spirit of the vote for women priests taken at General Synod in November. By making special arrangements by way of extra bishops to accommodate those who do not accept women priests, some of whom have spoken openly of 'taint', the bishops are tacitly agreeing to a point of view we believe to be offensive and indefensible, one which would not be tolerated in a racial context. Interestingly, when a similar idea was proposed in the McLean Report in 1986, Synod was so unhappy about it that the House of Bishops produced a new Report of their own rejecting the idea. What has changed the picture in the meantime is the threat by those opposed to create 'no-go areas', the further threat of large defections to Rome, and the financial anxieties that surround the cost of large scale compensations. We are concerned that no-go areas would cause deep distress, and that it would be very sad as well as very costly if many priests left the Church, but we do not see that threat can be a reason to deny important principles agreed by Synod, and in particular the principle that women can be priests. In short we do not accept that these 'two legitimate positions' or 'integrities' can be given the equal weight within the Church of England implied by the Act of Synod, and we think the Church is paying a price that is unacceptably high in a desperate attempt to achieve togetherness. We believe the Synod should not vote for the Act of Synod in November.

This letter was signed by four hundred people, some of them clergy but the majority of them lay. Only a handful of senior clerics signed. In view of this, it seems interesting that it says at the bottom of the advertisement that it is paid for by the signatories, and *also by those who agreed with the letter but felt unable to sign*. In private a number of clergy said that they feared for their livelihoods if they signed it.

Those who opposed the Act sometimes found themselves unpopular even among those who supported women's ordination. There was a feeling abroad, perhaps due to exhaustion or boredom, that having swallowed the gnat of the Measure, those in favour might as well strain to swallow the camel of the Act – women must be ordained at any price. The Movement for the Ordination of Women, intolerably stressed between wanting to see women ordained and the impossibility of the Act, turned to trusted clerical advisers who urged them not to oppose it. By the time of the debate MOW had begun to change its mind, but by then it was too late for its influence to make any impact. I remember vainly pleading the idea that the longest way round is sometimes the shortest way home, that for women to refuse ordination on such shabby terms might be very effective, even if it delayed things another year or two. I did not find many takers.

The mood of Synod in the debate about the Act was a strange one. The Archbishop of Canterbury did not speak at all, while the Archbishop of York, John Habgood, had a good deal to say and was clearly the mastermind of the whole project. The Bishop of Ely, Stephen Sykes, had given theological credence to the Act. What many of the speeches on the day parrotted was the upbeat charismatic vocabulary from the bishops' statements – of generosity, compassion, unity, of the spirit of Anglican compromise. There was no sense of apology to women, indeed they were barely mentioned. I was biassed against the Act, of course, but as I listened to the debate I felt a strong sense of a wistful people troubled about what they were being asked to approve, yet trying to be loyal to their bishops, who were, after all, so remarkably united. Looking down from the gallery on many bishops who had promised support in the past I wondered if their hearts could possibly be in the Act of Synod. 'Why *should* I vote for this?' one woman speaker, a newcomer to Synod, asked. 'If you don't', the Archbishop of York replied, picking up a nautical image just used by another speaker, 'you will sink the ship!'

Only a couple of speakers seemed ready to state unequivocally that principle might matter more than pragmatism – the Revd Bernice Broggio, who said that she felt unable to vote for something which would be illegal in the rest of society, and

Canon Philip Crowe, then Principal of Salisbury and Wells Theological College, who made the finest speech of the afternoon. Almost alone among the speakers he recognized that the debate was a discussion 'about the nature of the Church of England and whether there are any limits to tolerance, whether we reach a point where tolerance ceases to be a virtue and becomes a vacuum'. He suggested that the contradictions of the Act would make it ultimately unworkable, and quoted a Roman Catholic writer, Clifford Longley, observing the Act from outside, who used a telling simile for the double-think about women priests. 'There may be many Members of Parliament who hold that John Major should not be Prime Minister, but were they to hold that actually he is not Prime Minister they could hardly continue to operate in the same parliamentary system.' Philip Crowe said that he was ashamed to be part of a Synod passing such an Act. 'You'll never work in the Church of England again,' someone remarked to him afterwards, knowing that Salisbury Theological College was soon to be closed. This prophecy turned out to be true. In the willed climate of enthusiasm for the Act it was heresy to speak against it, rather like being a conscientious objector in time of war.

A small group of women and men protested when the Act was passed (overwhelmingly) by Synod, holding up banners spelling out 'Shame' and softly chanting the word. They were ejected from Synod amid cheers.

Even the longest river winds somewhere safe to sea, and the vocation of women as priests, despite dams and rocks and whirlpools of scorn, neglect, and Acts of betrayal, finally reached fulfilment in the ordinations celebrated all over the country in 1994, in some of the most joyful liturgies most of us have ever been privileged to share. The loving enthusiasm of clergy and laity who took part went some way to take away the taste of the dreadful period after the vote. Lesley Bentley's figures and description show just how firmly integrated women now are into church structures, which is also a way of saying how excellently they have worked. I believe she understates the quiet courage needed by women like herself to continue to work the present structure. 'It is harder', she remarks mildly, 'in areas where there is a concentration of parishes opposed to women's ordination.'

Yet as she says, there are opponents still talking as if 'we are still in a process of discernment' and suggesting that, if they play their cards right, they will get rid of women altogether. Not to mention clergy talking of the setting up of a Third Province for those opposed to women.

The Act opened a door to precisely this form of misunderstanding, a door which, as some of our contributors suggest, dangerously echoes the Donatist heresy, in which Christian minorities took it upon themselves to decide which leaders they would obey and grant authority to, and which they would not. Apart from the refusal among some to recognize the authority of women who are priests, anecdotal evidence also suggests that diocesan bishops are, in some cases, being ignored and sidelined in their own dioceses. John Baker writes of the damage already done to the catholicity of the church and the tragic loss of confidence in the Anglican tradition. Ian Jackson, a Methodist minister, wonders how on earth it is possible for the Methodists to have meaningful conversations with a church so at odds with itself as to produce the Act of Synod. 'Methodists looked with amazement at the Church of England, which voted so overwhelmingly to affirm the principle of ordaining women to the presbyteral ministery, and then turned itself inside out trying to mitigate the consequences of this for those who were so decisively outvoted . . . (it) seems like the maintenance of communion at the cost of an extraordinary sleight of mind. If this is what catholicity means to the Church of England it is not what it means to Methodists.'

So what can the future hold? At Synod in July 1998 it was announced that the House of Bishops had set up a group under the chairmanship of the Bishop of Blackburn to review the operation of the Act of Synod. It appears to be confining itself to the 'pastoral and practical considerations of the Act', i.e. not its theology, and 'there is no expectation that the review will result in proposals to rescind the Act'. So the unity of the church will continue to be flouted, women will continue to be treated as a source of 'taint' (like my friend in the opening paragraph), and other churches will continue to look on appalled as the Church of England fails to grasp the nettle of conflict, lives complaisantly with its own weakness and disunity, and continues to discriminate against women. It is a melancholy prospect. There is a huge loss of what might have been. 'The ordination of women to the priesthood', writes Jane Shaw, 'offered the church the opportunity to live as the Body of Christ in a distinctive way, distinguished not by our operation as human beings in terms of gendered stereotypes and prejudices, but rather by life in the Body of Christ.' For the time being that opportunity is lost.

It is surely time to consider rescinding such a hasty, misconceived, botched, discriminatory, divisive and theologically unsound piece of legislation as the Act of Synod. Bishop Baker writes: 'If our church is serious about its catholicity, one of its priorities should be to amend Clause I of the Act.' Such a change is by no means impossible. As one of the contributors remarks, 'What Synod made, Synod can unmake.'

I do not know if all the contributors to this book would want to go so far. Those most intimately connected with its working are less vociferous, I notice, than those of us more theoretically engaged, I hope because the goodness and kindness of actual Christians at the grass roots manages to soften and sweeten the damaging implications of the Act into something more kindly and human. It is part of the mystery of Christianity that the faithful frequently show love in surprising circumstances, and I am glad that it is so. But it is also important that the structures themselves do not make a scandal of the law of love. 'On balance there is evidence that serious attempts have been made to make the Act work in practice, but the central aim of preserving unity and dialogue has suffered in the detail of those attempts,' writes Lesley Bentley. 'In particular the Act appears to have opened the way to increasing isolation of those opposed to the ordination of women, or at least of one particular group of those so opposed. Communion is thereby lessened.'

Gender and the Act of Synod

JANE SHAW

By the enactment of the Priests (Ordination of Women) Measure 1993, and its associated Canons, the Church of England has opened the order of priests to women. This entails that the order is a single whole and that women duly ordained priest share equally with their male counterparts the exercise of its ministry, in synodical government and in consideration for suitable appointments.

> Priests (Ordination of Women) Measure 1993
> Code of Practice, 1

Passed by the General Synod to make provision for the continuing diversity of opinion in the Church of England as to the ordination and ministry of women as priests, and for related matters.

> Preamble to the Episcopal Ministry Act of Synod 1993

Two dominant and damaging views of gender relations operate in the church and Western society today. First, there is an old hierarchical view of humanity in which woman is seen as an inferior version of man, with man standing as the norm; secondly, there is a more modern and dualistic view of humanity in which men and women are seen as essentially different from each other, and are often thought in that 'difference' to display 'complementarity'. The first assumes that women and men are the same but unequal, while the second rhetorically asserts that women and men are different but equal, but operates in such a way that women and men are seen as different but *unequal*. Both views can be – and have been – sustained by scripture and tradition. Both can be problematic and dangerous for women and men – but especially for women –

because they operate according to various stereotypes of what it means to be a 'man' or 'woman', the consequences of which will be explored in more depth shortly.

I suggest here that while the decision to ordain women was ostensibly couched in terms of *equality*, whereby 'women duly ordained priest share equally with their male counterparts in the exercise of its ministry, in synodical government and in consideration for suitable appointments', the provisions made in the Act of Synod (and in the Code of Practice for the Priests (Ordination of Women) Measure[1]) to accommodate 'for the continuing diversity of opinion in the Church of England as to the ordination and ministry of women as priests' work to undermine that equality. The accommodating provisions do this by working sometimes alternately, and sometimes simultaneously, with the two models of gender relations outlined above. The old hierarchical model of humanity is used in such a way that man – for which we can read 'priest' – is seen as the norm, and thereby woman – for which we can read 'woman priest' – is necessarily seen as the inferior version of the norm, which is man. The modern 'different and complementary' model generally assumes that certain 'natural' differences exist between men and women, not least biological differences, and that this fits women and men for different or 'complementary' vocations. I conclude by suggesting that neither of these models is helpful for women and men, lay and ordained, in their work in the church and the world. These models of gender relations, and the stereotypes of humanity with which they operate, are not effective proclamations of the Incarnate God. Rather, we need an understanding of gender which acknowledges sexual difference but construes it in such a way that gifts rather than gender stereotypes are our starting point.

The hierarchical model

The hierarchical view of gender, stemming from the ancient world, remained remarkably persistent until the modern era, for up until the Enlightenment, the vast majority of people – including scientists and anatomists – relied upon the commentaries of Aristotle and Galen (and popularized versions of them). These taught that woman was an imperfect version of man. They believed that there was 'one sex', as the historian Thomas Laqueur expresses it, which was hierarchically arranged, with man as the perfect model, and therefore 'on top,' so to speak, and woman as the imperfect model.[2] In short, the very idea of sexual difference was not conceptualized. This notion of man as the 'norm' fitted with the second account of the creation of humankind in Genesis (2. 21–3). Eve or 'woman' was formed from the rib (or 'side') of Adam (that is, 'man'), while he was in a deep sleep. In this account woman was created as a helper for man, for it was not good for man to be alone (Gen. 2. 18). God split Adam in two, and thus woman was the other half of man; this suggests the creation of an androgynous Adam initially which came to be split into 'man' and 'woman'.

This hierarchical notion of gender was a part of the hier-archical nature of all pre-modern societies in the West, from the Roman household and state, appropriated by the early church, to the Puritan household of early modern England. The *order* of society was both hierarchical and patriarchal: man as master/husband/father was at the top, and servants, wives and children were hierarchically arranged below him. In this, the household (which was not the private family of the modern era) mirrored the state.

Scientifically, we no longer believe that women are inferior versions of men, and yet the attitude which regards man as 'the norm' prevails in much of society, but particularly within the church. The provisions for accommodating 'the continuing diversity of opinion in the Church of England as to the ordina-tion and ministry of women as priests' *necessarily* work with the hierarchical model of gender because such provisions are not so much designed to accommodate 'the continuing diversity of opinion', as the Act of Synod claims. Rather they are aimed solely at keeping within the fold of the Church of England (one might argue at whatever cost) those opposed to the ordination of women as priests.

With regard to this issue, there are two main groups within the church of England: the first group consists of those who are in favour of the ordination of women who accept both women and men priests, and the second of those who do not accept the ordination of women as priests. For this second group the norm of priesthood will always be male. As the provisions of the Act of Synod (and the Measure itself) are aimed at accommodating this second group, those provisions will necessarily work with a hierarchical model of gender. Man – 'priest' – is the norm; woman – 'woman priest' – is not. (The popular propensity to call men who are ordained 'priests' and women who are ordained 'women-priests' or 'lady-priests' illustrates this point.) Hence the two integrities set up by the Act of Synod can never be held *equally* side by side.

This can be seen in the reception of the Act of Synod, and the attempt to hold the two integrities together. Let me illustrate this with an example. At one Anglican theological college which aims, indeed claims, to hold the two integrities equally, one Mass a week is celebrated by a woman. On that same day, a second Mass is held for those men who cannot accept the ordination of women as priests. On the other days of the week, all Masses are celebrated by men and, as three out of the four (all male) ordained members of the college's staff are opposed to the ordination of women, a majority of those other Masses are necessarily celebrated by male priests who are opposed to the ordination of women to the priesthood. However, on those days, no alternative Mass is held for those men and women who are in favour of the ordination of women. For the two integrities to be held equally, it would be necessary, surely, to have Masses celebrated by women or men in favour of women priests on each day that a priest opposed to the ordination of women presided at the daily college Mass. It would be argued by many that such a move would not be necessary because those in favour of the ordination of women as priests do not question the orders of any male priests, be they in favour of or against the ordination of women as priests. Hence they can accept the validity of any Mass. And yet, this solution of 'matching

Masses' would be the only way of genuinely fulfilling the Act of Synod's general injunction that 'all concerned should endeavour to ensure that the integrity of differing beliefs and positions concerning the ordination of women to the priesthood should be *mutually* recognised and respected' (my italics).[3] Because one group within the church accepts the orders of all priests in the church, while the second group only accepts the order of male priests, such *mutual* recognition and respect can never exist, and genuinely equal provisions are not seen as necessary for both groups.

The very provision of Provincial Episcopal Visitors (hereafter referred to as PEVs), or 'flying bishops' as they are popularly called, each of whom is called to work 'in enabling extended pastoral care and sacramental ministry' and to 'act as spokesman and adviser for those who are opposed'[4] is a further illustration of this point in itself. Male priests and members of the laity who work with the old hierarchical model that 'priest' *necessarily* means 'male-priest' received their own special provision for upholding that view in the creation of PEVs. Frankly put, this is the institutionalization of sexism *par excellence*. It is also the inscription into synodical law of man as norm and woman as non-norm. I shall have more to say about PEVs in a moment, but want first to turn to the development of ideas of difference in the modern era.

'Difference' and complementarity

Notions of sexual difference – that is, that there are two distinctly different sexes, 'man' and 'woman' – first began to prevail in the Enlightenment, and not primarily because of any real scientific discoveries. For example, as Laqueur makes clear, the relevant discoveries about the significance of ovulation in women were not made until well into the nineteenth century.[5] Rather, there was an increasing need, socially and politically, to differentiate women from men. As Laqueur puts it, no one was interested in looking at the anatomical and concrete physiological differences between men and women until it became politically important to do so, in the late eighteenth century. This shift in thought about sex and gender occurred in the context of a new political discourse about rights and equality, prompted by both Enlightenment philosophy and the French Revolution. Some women, most famously Mary Wollstonecraft, agitated for the inclusion of women in the new calls for rights, but no one seriously considered giving women political and civil rights, even though the question was opened up. As the historian Londa Schiebinger puts it, 'How were Enlightenment thinkers to justify the inequality of women in the newly envisioned democratic order?'[6] The answer was what Thomas Laqueur calls the 'two-sex' model – that is, that women and men were to be understood as fundamentally different from each other. It was believed that the new science, thought to be objective and impartial, could provide the evidence to resolve this question about women's physical and intellectual character, and could define what the 'difference' might be. Of course, cultural and social ideas necessarily affected those supposedly 'natural' differences between the sexes.[7]

While some argued that women and men were equal but different, those differences were defined in such ways that, in practice, women were treated as different but *unequal*. Furthermore, the notion of sexual difference led to the idea of 'complementarity' whereby men and women were perceived as having different traits and characteristics which 'complement' each other. This notion of 'complementarity', often assumed to be a good thing, is particularly dangerous because it assumes a person has certain 'natural' characteristics solely on the basis of whether she or he is female or male. In practice, those characteristics which women have been assumed to display (home-keeping, nurturing, mothering, etc.) have been given less public value than the characteristics thought to be displayed by, and the jobs thought appropriate for, men. Under the banner of 'different and complementary' women have been excluded from 'male' tasks and jobs and 'male' vocations, even when clearly called to them. This has happened in the modern West in part because of the development, via industrialization, of private and public spheres at just about the same time that notions of sexual difference, political equality and rights were developing. Hence women, at least middle-class women, have been understood to have characteristics which have suited them in particular for the home, and the private sphere.[8]

In Christian terms, this view of gender, or sexual difference, could be justified by the first account of the creation of humankind, in Genesis 1. 26–30, read along with Genesis 3. In Genesis 1. 26–30, 'Adam' is divided into two human beings, male and female, from the beginning: 'And God created the adam in His image, in the image of God, He created him, male and female, He created them.' These two humans have dominion over the earth. The inequality in that 'difference' is provided by woman's sin related in Genesis 3, in which Eve was tempted by the serpent, and in turn tempted Adam, to eat the fruit and disobey God; her punishment was pain in childbirth and subordination to her husband, along with expulsion from the Garden of Eden with Adam.

Modern notions of the equality of women and men, which have been developed primarily within feminism (itself a product of the Enlightenment) have almost always been intertwined with notions of sexual 'difference'. For feminists were writing in an intellectual and social context in which they assumed that women and men were different but they wanted to argue that women and men were, nevertheless, genuinely equal. Feminism has therefore long grappled with this problematic of 'difference' leading the French feminist philosopher, Luce Irigaray, to claim that 'Sexual difference is one of the major philosophical issues, if not the issue, of our time.'[9] Certainly this difference remains a major cultural preoccupation – one might even say obsession – in the West, and sexual difference has frequently been privileged over other differences, for example, those concerning race and class. I shall return to some of these issues in the conclusion.

But what does any of this have to do with the ordination of women to the priesthood and the Act of Synod? It seems to me that older notions of gender hierarchy have melded with notions of sexual difference to create a fairly deadly mix in which women are simultaneously thought to be *both* the 'non-norm', as I have termed it, *and* different. One illustration of this can be found in the ways that the implementation of the Act of Synod's provisions have led to certain illogicalities and a 'theology of taint'. The refusal of those male priests who are opposed to the ordination of women to receive communion from bishops who have ordained women, and from priests who have concelebrated with or even received from women, has led to a 'theology of taint' which is deeply reminiscent of Donatist attitudes in the early church. The provision of PEVs has led to situations in which male priests, having received their holy orders from the Archbishop of Canterbury, now find themselves unable to receive communion from him, or in situations in which they may be ordained by a PEV but would make their oath of allegiance to the diocesan bishop, from whom they refuse to receive communion. What is the understanding of women in this 'theology of taint'? The logic behind it is that of gender hierarchy: namely, man/priest is the norm, while woman is not. But the effect – that is the 'theology of taint' which is a part of the reception (one might say ideological outworking) of the Act of Synod – relies upon a notion of woman as utterly different, nay untouchable. Here, woman may be equal in all other regards but her 'difference' discards her into a space which makes her sacramental ministry literally – for some – polluting. In this view, once touched by hands which have laid hands on a woman, one is tainted.

We might liken this notion of taint to the various taboos about menstruating women which exist in several religious traditions, including Christianity. For example, in some Eastern Orthodox churches today, women are discouraged from receiving communion while they are menstruating. And there are Eastern Orthodox priests who want to avoid being touched by menstruating women because of the 'taint' or pollution that such a touch conveys.

Mary Douglas, in her influential cross-cultural study, *Purity and Danger*, examined beliefs about pollution and taboo in a

wide range of religions and cultural systems to show how such
concepts 'carry a symbolic load' about danger, boundaries,
status and disorder.[10] If we analyse the notions of 'taint' which
have developed as the Act of Synod has been in reception (that
is, how it has worked in practice) in terms of Douglas' argument, then those ideas of 'taint' represent a fear of disorder, a
disorder which symbolizes both danger and power. The disorder symbolizes danger in that women priests are thought
to represent a rupture in either the apostolic succession or
scriptural authority (depending upon whether the opponent to
women priests is high or low church). And yet that disorder
represents power too: the very existence of the provisions of the
Act of Synod speak to the symbolic power of the ordination of
women to the priesthood. Such provisions are an attempt to
bring order to a situation which is perceived as disordered. And
yet this is ironic for at least two reasons. First, the provisions of
the Act of Synod have catered to the need for order amongst a
small sub-section of the church (that is, those opposed to the
ordination of women) but, in fact, the reception of the Act of
Synod has caused disorder within the church, not least ecclesio-
logically, but in a variety of other ways too, as illustrated by the
contributions to this book. Secondly, the disorder created by the
provisions and reception of the Act of Synod directly contra-
dicts one of the stated intentions of the Measure, which was to
entail that 'the order [of priests] is a single whole'.

Gender, society, tradition and the church

Questions about gender are necessarily caught up in a larger set
of issues about the relationship of the church to society, and
thus with ecclesiological matters. Some would claim that the
Church of England's decision to ordain women to the priesthood broke with scripture and tradition, and was a mark of its
capitulation to society. In fact, as I have illustrated, albeit
briefly, Christianity's notions of gender have always been
affected by (and have affected) society's ideas about gender, for
gospel and culture are always related, and always affect each

other. The roots of Christianity lie in an historically located and culturally shaped event, namely, the incarnation. Some Christians, who understand the church as a separate and gathered society of 'pure' Christianity, would deny this intertwining of gospel and culture and find refuge in notions of gender which they regard as somehow peculiarly 'Christian' but which in fact are culturally constructed.

The Church of England, as the established church, has by contrast always operated out of an incarnational ecclesiology, believing that it has as its mission something to offer to the whole people of God; something to say and do about the conditions of the world – injustice, poverty, prejudice and the mundane ins-and-outs of daily life – *and* the call to listen to God's people, for in their experiences and lives will be found the image and likeness of God and the movement of the Holy Spirit. Indeed, it has always made central a trinitarian doctrine of God in which the Holy Spirit is understood to be that part of God which effects change in the world, disturbing and disrupting us, and calling us to participate in a living and changing tradition.

The Church of England's attempt to 'make provision for the continuing diversity of opinion . . . as to the ordination and ministry of women as priests' via the Act of Synod has worked against its own incarnational ecclesiology and living tradition. For it has enshrined into law the (minority) opposition to the priesthood of women. This could hamper the movement of the Spirit and the proper development of the priesthood, in the continuing process of exchange between gospel and culture which is what makes the tradition a truly living and fully trinitarian tradition. It also counteracts the claim, made in the Code of Practice for the Measure, that the opening of the order of priests to women 'entails that the order is a *single whole* and that women duly ordained priest share equally with their male counterparts . . .' (my italics). How can the order be a 'single whole' when so many exceptions, based on notions of gender hierarchy and sexual difference, are prescribed by law?

An obvious example here is the Measure's failure to include the possibility of women as bishops. If we accept that the tradition is a living tradition, in which the church, in its historic continuity, nevertheless 'makes church' anew for each generation, then we can recognize that the inclusion of women in the episcopate might well be a development of the episcopacy consequent on the decision to ordain women to the diaconate and presbyterate. The inclusion of women in the episcopate would not simply be a radical move to please women, but part of a larger and ever-continuing process of re-shaping the role and function of bishops as occurs in every generation. In the exercise of oversight (*episkope*) an Archbishop Anselm is necessarily different from that of an Archbishop Cranmer, or Temple, or Carey. Similarly so with diocesan bishops. That is, the role and function change while the title and symbolism remain the same, or similar.[11]

The problem we encounter in both the Measure's Code of Practice and in the Act of Synod is that certain notions about gender form *the* guiding issues, and are taken as *the* starting point. The ordination of women to the priesthood offered the church the opportunity to live as the Body of Christ in a distinctive way, distinguished not by our operation as human beings in terms of gendered stereotypes and prejudices, but rather by life in the Body of Christ with Jesus Christ as the head. The entry of women into the priesthood promised that the order might at last be 'a single whole' so that a person's ministry would not be marked solely by their gender, and by the preconceived notions of what it means to be a 'man' or 'woman'. The entry of women into the priesthood promised that people might minister *according to their gifts*, and that the church might flourish by the fruits of such ministry in a more creative dynamic.

However, by passing legislation for the ordination of women to the priesthood in such a way that gender would remain an issue (and here I think we can point particularly to the Act of Synod), those hopeful and liberating possibilities have become more complicated and compromised. In this, the Church of England is seriously out of step with society. As I have suggested, some Christians – believing in a gathered church set apart from the world – would find that attractive, but the incarnational ecclesiology of the Church of England embraces rather a notion of church which both affects and is affected by the world and which incorporates the experiences and lives of the human beings (made in the image and likeness of God) to whom it pastors. To be so seriously out of step with society, in allowing discrimination against women who work for the church, in enshrining in law damaging notions of sexual difference and gender hierarchy, hampers the proclamation of the incarnate God. Or, as Bishop Penny Jamieson puts it, 'Why is the church the only place where women, *on principle*, are excluded from certain jobs? Isn't this the sign of a deeply unhealthy church?'[12]

As I noted earlier, sexual difference and its possible meanings have been much debated in the modern era by both feminists and non-feminists. Feminists have asked how we might understand men and women as different but equal, some arguing that there are certain 'natural' differences (physiological, psychological) between the sexes which must be respected, and others arguing that if such differences do exist, they are so overlaid with cultural assumptions that we cannot possibly understand either what those differences might be or their significance for gender relations.

Problems and conflicts about the meaning of sexual difference seem to arise when that difference is construed as oppositional – that is, only in terms of the opposition of 'masculine' and 'feminine' – rather than relational. Once we understand sexual difference as relational, we can stop supposing that some 'essential' thing makes all women somehow alike, in opposition to another 'essential' thing which makes all men somehow alike. We can also take other differences (such as ethnic and racial and class differences) into account, and use as a starting point the gifts of a person in their particular context, for not all women are going to display the same gifts in the priesthood, just as all men do not display exactly the same gifts in their ministry. The anthropologist Henrietta Moore writes that at this time, while gender is such a fraught and complicated issue, 'we might be better off working back towards sex, gender, sexual difference and the body, rather than taking them as a set of starting point.'[13] What we might learn from this comment by Moore is that instead of beginning with our presuppositions about what it means to be a man or a woman, we might bracket those presuppositions initially and begin with the person, the gifts, the vocation and work towards (rather than from) what it means for a particular *woman* or *man* to be a priest.

Now that we have ordained women to the priesthood, our starting point for discussions of the priesthood might therefore begin not with gender, but with vocation and gifts. Of course, this happens in some parts of the church. But the institutionalization of opposition to the ordination of women to the priesthood does not merely set the odds against this happening, but acts against it. It also means that the actions of the Holy Spirit, and the gifts and vocations which are of the Holy Spirit, might be seriously limited. For gifts and vocations are not tied to one's gender (nor, for that matter, to body or race) although of course they are experienced and put into practice in contexts which are shaped by our understandings of gender (and by body and race). The institutionalization of opposition to women priests betrays a materialist attitude and a lack of confidence in the Spirit. For it is in understanding priesthood primarily in terms of gifts that we embrace the Spirit, and begin to enact God's will. And it is in that way that we continue to grow as a living, vibrant and fully trinitarian church.

2

A Theological Reflection – The Lost Anglican Tradition

JOHN AUSTIN BAKER

When this Act was discussed in General Synod in November 1993, and voted upon, I had already retired, and so took no part in that debate. I was, however, involved as a member of the House of Bishops with the drafting of the Act, and with the document, *Bonds of Peace*, which set out some of the thinking behind the Act, and which I had been unable to support when it was agreed by the House in Manchester in June of the same year. But the present chapter is in no way an attempt to recall or refurbish those 'old, unhappy far-off things, and battles long ago'. What I have tried to do is to reflect afresh from a theological standpoint on the text of the Act five years on. In the course of doing so, however, it has seemed unavoidable to touch on some collateral matters; and the conclusion of my thoughts will raise one or two points of more general concern.

The Preamble to the Act

At first glance the Preamble to the Act might seem of no particular theological significance. It is natural to read it as an expression of pastoral intent, of kindly concern for fair play and mutual respect within the Body of Christ; and this it undoubtedly is. Unfortunately it is also far more of a logical and theological chaos than I appreciated at the time.

A preliminary point concerns the whole nature of the Act. The opening lines of the Preamble define its purpose. It was the

General Synod's mind 'to make provision for the continuing diversity of opinion in the Church of England as to the ordination and ministry of women as priests'. In sub-paragraph 1 of the next section, however, it notes that 'The Church of England through its synodical processes has given final approval to a Measure to make provision by Canon for enabling women to be ordained to the priesthood.' There is a contradiction here which is fundamentally destructive throughout the Act.

In the first passage quoted the belief that women may properly be ordained as priests and the belief that they may not are given equal status as 'diversities of opinion'. But the second passage states the plain fact that the Church of England has decided, by full constitutional process, that women may be so ordained, and has given authority to its bishops to do so. This position, therefore, ceases to be simply an opinion held by some church members. The Church's governing body, on behalf of the whole Church of England, has concluded that it is right for the Church *as a Church* to ordain women as priests. So far as the Church of England is concerned, therefore, the contrary view is not on a par with the official teaching, and should not be referred to as if it were.

This is no empty quibble about words. The phrasing of the Act betrays a failure to understand what is entailed theologically, for the life of any church, by a synodical decision made in waiting upon the guidance of the Holy Spirit. It treats the Church of England not as a church, an organic communion, but as a mere aggregation of Christians. What was really needed was an Act '*to make provision for protecting the rights of those in the Church of England who cannot accept the ordination of women as priests, and for their pastoral care*'.

This basic failure in understanding shapes the whole Act. It has, for example, determined the language of a later passage in the Preamble. Sub-paragraph (3. a. iii) reads: 'the integrity of differing beliefs and positions concerning the ordination of women to the priesthood should be mutually recognised and respected'. And indeed it should. No one, it is to be hoped, wants to deny the integrity either of those opposed to women's ordination or of those who support it. But a person's integrity tells one nothing about the truth or falsity of the beliefs they hold. What is at issue is not who is righteous, but who is right.

The phrase, 'the two integrities', was widely used at the time, and continues to be so. But in a rather slithery way it tends to mean different things to different people or at different moments. Sometimes it denotes no more than the honourable sincerity of both sides in their divergent convictions. But at other times it acquires overtones of validity: that the belief and practice of the Church of England can be validly determined by each of the two ways simultaneously. Thus, *Bonds of Peace* refers not just to the integrity but to the 'legitimacy' of both positions.[1] But that simply cannot be so; and to pretend that it can simply plunges one into the logical shambles which always results from saying 'Yes' and 'No' at the same time.

An idea put forward, as I recall, at the July 1993 General Synod by the Bishop of Ely will help to make this point clear. He argued that by the measures proposed Anglicanism could take into its own life the divisions that already existed between churches, and from experiencing the pain of these conflicts in its own daily existence work more wholeheartedly to find ways of resolving them, not just internally but ecumenically. This was a noble aspiration, but is it theologically sustainable?

To refuse recognition to the ministers of another ecclesial body does indeed give pain. Anglicans have inflicted this pain often enough on others, and are themselves equally often on the receiving end where, for example, co-operation with Catholics or Orthodox is involved. Today friendly courtesy has widely replaced the cold dismissiveness of yesteryear, and with studied care churches give qualified theological approval to the ordained ministries of others; and these are, at the human level, improvements. But the essential pain is still there. 'You' are not an authentic priest/bishop as 'I' am. The sacraments 'you' celebrate may be means of grace, but they are not fully what God intends, whereas 'ours' are.

Theologically this is the crux. Where ministries are not

recognized, full sacramental fellowship cannot exist; and where full sacramental fellowship is not present, you cannot have one church. That is the acid test. Certainly you may have sacramental fellowship and mutual recognition of ministries between two groups of Christians which still agree for various reasons to go on living as two distinct ecclesial bodies. But where you do not have fellowship and recognition you cannot have one ecclesial body. When, therefore, within the Church of England so called, one section refuses to recognize ministers officially ordained and appointed, or to have sacramental fellowship with them, then by all normal theological criteria they are saying, 'We do not belong to the same church.' As the General Synod's Board for Mission and Unity trenchantly expressed it: 'The Church cannot be seen to be one unless its ordained ministry is seen to be one.'[2]

Refusal to recognize women ordained as bishops makes this even clearer, because the bishop is both the fount of holy order within his or her jurisdiction, and the chief president in the eucharistic fellowship. The charitable hope of the Bishop of Ely would seem to lead simply into a theological impasse.

The same applies to that concept invoked by the Eames Commission, and widely welcomed, namely 'impaired communion'. That there can be such a thing is undoubtedly true. But where one Christian minister, say, refuses to take part in the ordination of another, or to receive communion at a eucharist where that minister presides or even where he or she is a fellow communicant, there is not 'impaired' communion but no communion at all.[3] Those who reject the decisions of their church in such matters have withdrawn from communion with it, and thus *de facto* if not *de jure* have constituted themselves a separate ecclesial body.

When, therefore, the Preamble to the Act goes on to say that 'all concerned should endeavour to ensure that . . . the highest possible degree of communion should be maintained within each diocese' (3.a.ii), it is asking for something which, in any genuinely theological use of the word 'communion', is an impossibility. The only wording that could have been used with theological integrity would have been as follows: '. . . *to ensure that all possible steps are taken within each diocese to maintain dialogue in charity with those opposed to this decision, and to encourage them to return to full communion with other members of the Church of England*'. So far as the present situation is concerned, the most that can be claimed is the degree of unity which exists between all the baptized, a unity of fundamental importance, certainly, but, as the history of ecumenical relations shows, not one which has as yet given rise to much practical effect.

This brings us to another major puzzle in the Preamble. Sub-paragraph (3.a.i) reads as follows: 'all concerned should endeavour to ensure that discernment in the wider Church of the rightness or otherwise of the Church of England's decision to ordain women to the priesthood should be as open a process as possible'.

What is actually envisaged here? The words quoted suggest something like a 'dialogue' by which other churches are helped to understand the thinking behind the ordination of women to the priesthood in the Church of England, and to pass judgment upon it. But they also seem to imply that if that judgment proves to be negative it might be the duty of the Church of England – and presumably of other Provinces in the Anglican Communion – to reverse that decision. Indeed, it is hard to see what other meaning can be attached to those words, 'or otherwise'. Thus, during the debate leading up to the crucial Synod vote there were a number of references to the 'process of reception' (both internal and ecumenical) which would in time yield such a verdict.

To begin with, it is virtually impossible to imagine any reality which might correspond to these fine-sounding words. Are we to suppose that if after, say, a generation of ordaining women to the priesthood Catholics and Orthodox could still not be persuaded that such ordinations were right, the Church of England would turn round to its women priests, and say, 'We're terribly sorry, but it was all a dreadful mistake, and you never were priests after all'? Leaving aside the fact that, if this is seriously envisaged, it is hard to think of a more cruel way of devaluing the priesthood offered to our women, and of making it meaningless, to anyone with any knowledge at all of the history of ecumenical relations the whole idea is preposterous. Churches simply do not say that major decisions in their tradition, made under God and fundamental to their life, were wrong. We, as Anglicans, are as unlikely at some future date to say that the ordination of women as priests was wrong as to go back on the Reformation settlement. Progress towards closer communion comes by incorporating the past into frameworks of new and larger understanding.

But the present text conceals other theological confusions. There already are major Christian traditions – Methodist or Baptist or Reformed, for example – which ordain women. But when these are cited in support this is often countered by the objection that their doctrine of ministry is not the same as ours, because they reject the concept of a special ministerial priesthood, and that their support is therefore irrelevant. If that argument is valid, however, it is equally irrelevant to appeal to Orthodox or Roman Catholic approval or disapproval, since their doctrines of ministry also differ from ours in important particulars. It is easy for us as Anglicans to fall into the trap of supposing that, because we have kept the three historic orders of ministry, we mean by them the same as others who have done so. But the Roman Catholic Church, at any rate, has always been clear that we do not. Hence its refusal to recognize the validity of Anglican Orders, or to accept officially the findings of ARCIC I. For them, our ordination of women is not something which has fatally damaged a previously catholic doctrine of ministry but just additional proof that our doctrine is defective.

The Church of England does have its own understanding of ministerial priesthood, developed over the centuries from the Reformation to the present time by a continuous tradition of theological reflection.[4] This tradition agrees with that of the Roman Catholic Church on a number of points, such as the fact that priests form a 'college' in fellowship with their bishop, that they have a primary duty of preaching the gospel, of pastoral care, and of administering the means of grace, that they alone may preside at the eucharist but that they do so in union with all the people of God, that such presidency as well as blessing and absolution are reserved to them and the bishops alone, and that their priesthood, like that of all the laity, derives from the one supreme and perfect High Priesthood of Christ.

On other points, however, there are significant differences between the traditions, not least on matters specifically relevant to the ordination of women. For the Roman Church the fundamental argument against such ordination is the 'completely free and sovereign' decision of Christ himself, when he chose only men to be his apostles. For the Roman Church this is a 'perennial norm', followed by the apostles themselves 'when they chose fellow workers who would succeed them in their ministry'; and this choice has governed the practice of the Church ever since in appointing others to carry on the apostles' mission.[5]

The view of the Church of England on this matter is rather differently nuanced, giving greater weight in its judgment to historical considerations. The emergence of the threefold ministry is seen not so much in terms of direct and conscious succession, instituted by the apostles, but rather as something consonant with the apostolic teaching and mission, which came about in the early church in order to continue and safeguard these things. The attribution of a priestly character to this ministry was something that happened relatively soon in the church's story, but was not there from the beginning.[6] However firmly one may believe that the ministerial priesthood is something that has Christ's blessing upon it, it is not possible to say that it is of dominical institution.[7] Thus the Preface to the Ordering of Bishops, Priests and Deacons makes no mention of this, but says simply: 'It is evident unto all men diligently reading Holy Scripture and ancient Authors, that *from the Apostles' time*' (emphasis mine) 'there have been these Orders of Ministers in Christ's Church: Bishops, Priests and Deacons.' Likewise, in the Thirty-Nine Articles of Religion, Article XXV teaches plainly that orders are not a 'Sacrament of the Gospel', nor one of those ordained of Christ our Lord.

It is to be understood, therefore, that in the Anglican formularies and theological tradition the threefold ministry is an institution inspired by the Holy Spirit, the relevance of which to the ordination of women is that what the church has been guided by the Spirit to institute it may presumably be guided by the same Spirit to enlarge and amend as God's purposes unfold. The Lord's choice of men as apostles would also seem not to be prescriptive in this matter, in view of the fact that the first-generation apostles were a unique group in the church, and that the title of 'apostle' was never again applied to any church leader or minister.[8]

A further relevant feature in the Roman Catholic understanding of priestly ministry is the belief that in celebrating the eucharist the priest acts *in persona Christi*, and that it is therefore at least appropriate that the priest should be male. This view has become popularized in the form that 'the priest is an ikon of Christ', but the official Roman statements are considerably more careful and theologically precise. They may be summarized as follows: 'When the Church celebrates the Eucharist, . . . the sacrifice Christ offered once for all on the cross remains ever present . . . In the Eucharist Christ gives us the very body which he gave up for us on the cross, the very blood which he "poured out for many for the forgiveness of sins" . . . The Eucharist is thus a sacrifice because it *re-presents* (makes present) the sacrifice of the cross, because it is its *memorial* and because it *applies* its fruit.'[9] The eucharist, like all sacraments, is an action of Christ, adminstered by the agency of men.[10] 'The action of the consecrating priest is the very action of Christ, who acts through his minister'; 'the priest-celebrant puts on the person of Christ'.[11] He 'presides in the person of Christ'.[12]

The Anglican understanding does not go as far as these statements, but there is a strand within Anglican tradition in modern times, deriving from the Tractarians, that the priest in the eucharist does in some sense represent Christ. The sacrifice which Christ made once for all upon the cross he now eternally offers for us in his Father's presence in heaven. The priest or bishop offering the eucharistic prayer with the bread and wine makes a memorial which unites what the church does on earth with what Christ does in heaven, and therefore may be said to 'represent' Christ.[13] Using rather different language, ARCIC I says that in the eucharist the minister 'is seen to stand in sacramental relation to what Christ himself did in offering his own sacrifice'.[14]

There is a fine but definite line to be drawn between the eucharistic celebrant as 'representing' Christ and the concept of Christ's being personally present in the priest who is Christ's agent in the act of consecration. After all, one person can represent another without the person represented being spiritually present within the representative. What is not at all clear is why on either understanding our Lord would find it inappropriate or unfitting to choose a woman to represent him or to be his agent in this context, when he uses women as his representatives and agents in other areas of church life, such as ministry or mission. The use of the 'ikon' metaphor may have done a good deal to foster in people's minds an over-emphasis on the visual aspect of the matter, as may also the now almost universal practice of the celebrant's facing westward, with its evocation of the Last Supper in works of art. But, it may be asked, why, if the outward appearances of bread and wine bear no resemblance to the reality believed to be within them,[15] should the minister, as a sacramental representative of Christ as the celebrant, need to bear such a resemblance, and in one particular only?

It must also be remembered that the idea of the minister's representing Christ has come into prominence in Anglican reflection only because of the efforts over the last hundred and fifty years to find common ground with Roman doctrine. In the earlier stages of Anglican thinking the emphasis was where the Book of Common Prayer clearly lays it, namely on the priest as offering the prayers of the congregation and pleading the once-for-all sacrifice of Christ. The idea of the priest as in some special, quasi-sacramental relation to the person of Christ does not appear in the Book of Common Prayer or the Ordinal or the seventeenth-century divines. In this, their approach was in harmony with the whole liturgical tradition of christendom. For it is undeniable that in every liturgy known to us where the narrative of the Institution is included in the eucharistic prayer that narrative is related in the third person: 'who in the same night that *he* was betrayed, took bread, and gave you thanks . . .' But this simple fact makes it quite illogical to think of the celebrant acting and speaking *in persona Christi*. The Christian liturgical tradition is plainly one of the president offering the eucharist to the Father through Christ in the power of the Spirit on behalf of the congregation and the whole people of God. Anglicans would seem to be justified, therefore, in rejecting the very close and specific identification of the celebrant with Christ in the crucial eucharistic action, and with it the objection to women priests based upon it.

In the light of such considerations what are we to make of the Act's commendation of a process of ecumenical assessment of the Church of England's decision? Approval or disapproval of the ordination of women to the priesthood is bound to spring in any given church from the total understanding of ordained ministry in that church. If the Anglican understanding of ministry leaves room for the ordination of women where the Roman Catholic or Orthdox doctrine does not, then it is at that level of basic beliefs that dialogue has to be conducted, as it has been in a whole series of bilateral and worldwide ecumenical discussions.[16] But such processes require great theological resources, much prayer, and a lot of time and patience; and, moreover, each such dialogue affects the outcomes of all the others. To suggest that the Church of England can or should treat its ordination of women to the priesthood as in some sense provisional until those outcomes are known is simply, as people say, to be living on another planet. If it were felt that the Act ought to refer to this ecumenical dimension, then the most that should have been said in (3.a.i) would be some such statement as this: '*all concerned should endeavour to ensure that dis-cernment in the wider church of the reasons for the Church of*

England's decision to ordain women to the priesthood is encouraged by an open process of explanation and mutual understanding.'

The text of the Act

When we turn to the text of the Act, the very first clause, under the heading, 'Ordinations and Appointments', raises further theological questions:

> 1. Except as provided by the Measure and this Act no person or body shall discriminate against candidates either for ordination or for appointment to senior office in the Church of England on the grounds of their views or positions about the ordination of women to the priesthood.

On the face of it this is a fundamental safeguard for freedom of conscience, and as such it seems as if it would be utterly wrong to object to it. The use of the phrase 'discriminate against' subtly brands the actions in question as unethical. But on closer inspection the same fatal false step becomes evident which marked the opening words of the Preamble, namely the treatment of the Church of England's decision and the opinions of dissenting members or groups as if they were on a par. Of course, if they were, it would be a gross abuse to discriminate against anyone on either side on such grounds. But they are not.

Ordination is consecration for and incorporation into an 'order', a community of clergy bound together by a common calling and commission. The church which ordains each individual, and gives him or her a particular office and authority, has also seen fit to ordain all the others. All derive their priesthood (or diaconate or episcopate) from God through the one church to which they belong.

A word should perhaps be inserted here on a specific point. As is well known, candidates for priestly or episcopal ordination in the Church of England are not ordained as priests or bishops in that church only. They are presented 'to be ordained to the office of priesthood/bishop in the Church of God', and at the moment of ordination the bishop or metropolitan says, 'Send down the Holy Spirit upon your servant N for the office and work of a priest/bishop in your Church.' The implicit claim is that a person so ordained is qualified to be regarded as a priest or bishop in any other branch of the One, Holy, Catholic and Apostolic Church throughout the world, because the Church of England, together with the whole Anglican Communion, is itself a full part of that Church.[17] But if a priest, say, concludes that by some act his church has forfeited the right to be called 'catholic', then he is saying that its ordinations are, from a catholic standpoint, null and void, and he puts himself out of sacramental fellowship with the 'order' of which he was a member. This is precisely what numbers of objectors to the ordination of women as priests have done, for example, by boycotting chapter meetings, ordinations or chrism eucharists, and by demanding bishops of their own.

In the past, priests or bishops who sadly came to the conclusion that their orders received through the Anglican Church were, in fact, not valid catholic orders usually sought to be received into a church which they considered indubitably catholic, and to be ordained there. This was logical, because a priest without a church and an order is a contradiction in terms. But this is not the situation with which the Church of England is now faced. What the Act has done is to create two episcopates and two orders of priesthood, neither in communion with the other, within what is allegedly one church.

Some would argue, however, that the Anglican Communion is the one church in the Christian world with a way out of this absurdity. By the convenient doctrine of provincial autonomy it is open to individual Provinces within the Communion to decide for themselves whether to ordain women as priests or bishops, or to recognize women so ordained elsewhere. Hence the movement to seek a Third (non-geographical) Province within England, to which clergy and congregations opposed to the decision about women's ordination could belong. But theologically this is no solution at all. The fact that within the

Communion there are already Provinces, such as our own, which refuse Anglican women bishops from elsewhere the right to minister within their jurisdiction means that the Communion is at least very near to becoming simply a federation of churches with a common origin. The 'Third Province' solution only extends this process to the Church of England.

That is the situation in which Anglicans find themselves today; and it can be argued that, so far as the Church of England is concerned, the Act of Synod is simply one way, albeit an untidily complex one, of meeting an inescapable moral demand which that situation presents. The provision of episcopal care for dissenting clergy and laity, with which the remainder of the Act is concerned, has been subjected to a theological critique by Dr Judith Maltby elsewhere in this volume; and there is no need for me to repeat here the work she has done. But the reason for going down that road was that it was felt unjust to force either clergy or laity to uproot from the spiritual environment in which their lives had been spent, simply because they could not accept this major change which their church had made.

It was right to recognize this moral obligation, but not right to try to meet it by destroying the structure of catholic order within the Church of England, not even as a merely temporary expedient, but permanently. The Measure and the Code of Practice had already provided adequate and in some respects arguably excessive safeguards. The Act went further in two fatal respects. The first was to concede, as Dr Maltby has shown, the Donatist doctrine of 'taint'. The second was to go beyond the proper bounds of care for vested interests by seeking to ensure protection and provision for any who might oppose the Church of England's decision into an indefinite future.

The key clause here is the one with which we began our examination of the text of the Act, namely that concerning Ordinations and Appointments. A candidate for holy orders who is opposed to women's priestly ordination is declaring in advance that he has no intention of being in sacramental fellowship with the whole order into which he seeks to be admitted. Nor does he acknowledge that the very church to which he himself is looking for the gift of holy order has authority to ordain whomsoever, under God, it thinks fit. Both logically and theologically, to refuse such a candidate ordination is not to discriminate, for the simple reason that he has disqualified himself for the office he seeks.[18] If refusing such candidates ordination means, as it does, that in time the supply of clergy opposed to the decision must come to an end, that is the unavoidable consequence of fidelity to the catholic theology of ministry as the Church of England has always understood it. If our church is serious about its catholicity, one of its priorities should be to amend Clause 1 of the Act. When the day comes that the supply of dissenting priests and bishops is exhausted, then we must pray that those laity who still refuse to receive normal jurisdiction and ministry will recognize that sadly they ceased long since to be truly members of the Church of England, and will find a new church where they will feel more at home.

Postscript

There would seem to be two general lessons to be learned from this sorry history. The first is that the Church of England – and perhaps the Anglican Communion as a whole – seems to have lost confidence in its own Anglican theological tradition. The result is that decisions are assessed in the light of understandings of ordained ministry obtaining in other traditions. This was at least a very important aspect of what happened in the present case. Whatever the reasons, this tendency needs to be rectified urgently if Anglicanism is to regain a proper self-confidence and cohesion.

The second lesson concerns the extent to which individualism has permeated our church life. One theme of this chapter has been the way in which equal weight was accorded in the Act to the opinions of individuals and groups on the one hand, and to the solemn constitutional decisions of the church as a church on the other. Respect for justice and freedom of prayerful conscience are essential values. But so are respect for the corporate mind and action of the church, under the guidance of the Holy Spirit; and both are critical for true and effective Christian life and witness in the world.

In conclusion, I would simply want to stress one point. God's grace for God's work is given wherever souls sincerely trust in him. To be a lay person or deacon or priest or bishop in the Church of England does not cease to be a divine vocation and precious gift just because that church's theological structures may have got a bit muddled. Perhaps we might be more effective if they were not; but our Lord continues to use us all, and his Spirit will gradually guide us together into his truth.

3

One Lord, One Faith, One Baptism, but Two Integrities?

JUDITH MALTBY

Around 1980, I attended a Central Council meeting of the Movement for the Ordination of Women. One of the tasks set the meeting was to break into the inevitable small groups, armed with magic markers and newsprint, and 'buzz' about the reasons we thought that the Church of England should admit women to the priesthood. Bluetack in hand we then reported back to plenary. The vast majority of the reasons given, it is fair to say, had a great deal to do with the feelings of the people there: the deaconesses present felt frustrated that their gifts were not being fully employed; the male priests felt guilty that the same vocation they saw in themselves was being denied to their female colleagues; the women, both lay and the would-be ordained, felt that comparisons of the ordination of members of one half of the human race to the ordination of a monkey or a pork pie were, truth to tell, deeply insulting and unchristian. After awhile, a senior bishop present stood up and told us all, in a word, to stop whingeing. He said that the leadership of the church was not really interested in the *feelings* of women: we had to make an intellectually rigorous, *theological* case for why the Church of England should reform itself in this regard. I am to this day deeply grateful for the painful honesty of that bishop. The Movement for the Ordination of Women responded to the challenge and produced literature of a high theological content. Authors who published on the pro-side included Janet Morley, John Austin Baker, Rowan Williams,

Monica Furlong, and Elaine Storkey to name just a few. In an article published in 1984, Rowan Williams eloquently argued 'the case for theological seriousness', criticizing the lack of theological rigour in the ordination of women debate.

> The theology of Christian ministry is an area in which we are too readily tempted to avoid discussion of first principles. It is too complicated, too generally unsettling and too distracting when we are hard-pressed by practical urgencies . . . There are quite a few who would say that, at the moment, a theology of (ordained) ministry is neither possible, nor desirable: we have inherited a jumble of rather irrational structures and practices which we are slowly – and *pragmatically* – learning to adjust and rationalize or even modernize; and in this sort of situation we are inevitably going to treat all theological perspectives on the ministry as provisional.[1]

The ordination of women as priests has been subjected, very rightly, to intense rigour in terms of its theological *content* as well as wide consultation across international, national and the most local levels, of church government in terms of the *process* by which it was approved. My intention here is to apply some theological and intellectual rigour to the 1993 Act of Synod, and principally to the notion of extended episcopal oversight it embodies, as well as to the process by which it came into being. In short, this chapter sets out to ask some 'first principle' questions of the Act of Synod. It is not unjust to say that the Act has not undergone the searching testing which the ordination of women underwent. Nor, truth to tell, in the early years of the Act's existence did the cultural climate of the church encourage open criticism or dissent. This is in spite of the fact that for a growing number of Anglicans and other Christians, it is the Act and the novelty of Provincial Episcopal Visitors it created, not the ordination of women, which represents the *real* departure from a catholic understanding of orders and sacraments made by the Church of England in the late twentieth century. Some 'theological seriousness' on the Act is overdue and surely no one can object to the same rigour being applied: what is sauce for the goose is sauce for the gander. If 'theological seriousness' was good enough for the Measure, it is surely good enough, and overdue, for the Act of Synod.

Content

This chapter originally came into existence as a result of speaking with a group of bright, young, able ordinands, who simply had no idea about the conditions the 1992 Measure actually lays down for the ordination of women to the priest-hood. They had not even heard of the Act of Synod.[2] Alarmingly, there is a widespread perception in the Church of England, even among those with senior responsibility, that women are admitted to the ordained priesthood under the same conditions as men (a deeply inaccurate perception), and that the provisions made for the opponents of the ordination of women in the Act, which are additional to already extensive provisions made in the Measure, are one and the same. The 1992 Measure was debated at national and local levels of church life and stands on its own; the 1993 Act came into existence after the Measure was approved by the final vote by General Synod and is completely distinct from it. Given the level of ignorance surrounding both the Measure and the Act, it is worth going over precisely what each contains before considering the sharply contrasting processes by which each came into being.

The Provisions of the 1992 Measure

The main provisions of the Measure are as follows:
1. The ordination of women as priests but not on the same basis as male candidates.
2. Exemption of women clergy from any protection in law provided by the 1975 Sex Discrimination Act.
3. By passing either or both of Resolutions A and B, Parochial Church Councils may ban a woman priest from celebrating the eucharist or pronouncing the absolution

within parish boundaries, and are also given the right to prohibit the appointment of a duly ordained priest of the Church of England, or even from applyling for the post of incumbent, curate or non-stipendiary minister, on the basis of her sex. It is worth noting that PCCs were not given the right positively to request a woman rather than a man; there is no positive discrimination here, only 'negative discrimination'. Also one PCC in a united benefice can stop the appointment of a woman priest to minister anywhere else in the benefice, even if all the other parishes support her appointment. Further, there is no provision for the protection of the consciences of those in favour of women priests in a parish if Resolutions A and B are passed.

4. Financial provision was made for clergy who left as a consequence of the vote. No provision was made for the repayment of the sum of up to £30,000 if any, as a few have done, return.

5. The Measure explicitly excludes the ordination of women as bishops. The ordination of women to the episcopate will require an entirely distinct synodical measure and act of Parliament.

6. The Measure provides protection for bishops opposed to the ordination of women as priests by ensuring that no bishop could be 'forced' to ordain a woman to the priesthood.[3]

It is worth going over these points because one might reasonably conclude that the 1992 Measure contained a good deal of compromise and generous provision for those opposed. That was my view as I spoke for the Measure in deanery and other debates in 1990–91, sometimes not against opponents of women's ordination but against those who thought we had compromised too much.

The Provisions of the Act of Synod

The Act of Synod is, of course, a completely separate synodical act from the 1992 Measure. A measure is something that eventually is turned into a law – so the Measure had to be passed by Parliament and was, in November 1993, by large majorities. An Act of Synod simply has the authority of Synod and does not need to be referred to Parliament. An 'act' does not have the status of law in the same way and what Synod has made, Synod can unmake. The ordination of women Measure, however, would have to be repealed by Parliament, as well as by General Synod.

What are the main points of the 1993 Act of Synod?

1. The Act provides even greater 'protection' for those opposed to the ordination of women than the already extensive provision in the 1992 Measure outlined above.
2. The Act makes provision for neighbouring bishops of differing views on the ordination of women as priests to 'assist' each other. A bishop opposed is encouraged by the Act to call in a suffragan or neighbouring bishop to conduct the ordinations of women priests in his diocese. A bishop who supports women priests is encouraged to call for the assistance of an opposed neighbour to ordain men opposed and even to minister to congregations who feel they cannot accept their own bishop because of his support for the ordination of women.
3. The most significant aspect of the Act, however, is the creation of PEVs (Provincial Episcopal Visitors), or Flying Bishops as they were quickly dubbed by the press. PEVs appear to have largely, but not entirely, replaced the more co-operative model originally favoured in the Act as outlined in no. 2. This is 'Resolution C'.

As to the first point, *Bonds of Peace*, the supporting document to the Act, says this:

Those who for a variety of reasons cannot conscientiously accept that women may be ordained priests will continue to

hold a legitimate and recognised position within the Church
of England. There should be no marginalisation of anyone on
the basis of their attitude towards the ordination of women to
the priesthood. Nor should those who cannot accept the
ordination of women seek to marginalise themselves by with-
drawing from the life and government of the Church except
in those matters where conscientious convictions are directly
at stake.[4]

There are real questions as to whether either of these goals has
been helped by the Act of Synod, especially the injunction for
opponents not to withdraw 'from the life and government of the
Church'. The freewheeling nature of remarks like 'except in
those matters where conscientious convictions are directly at
stake' and the elevation of conscience over a catholic understanding of orders, is leading to some very dangerous consequences to which I will return later.

As for the second and third points, the provision of a 'safe
pair of hands', this is what the House of Bishops had to say:

The bishops, corporately and individually, are pledged to
maintain the integrity of both positions. Both are represented
in the House of Bishops. The House now indicates how in
practice the dioceses and the local churches can live with this
diversity. It will be a sign of the continuing communion of
bishops and a mark of collegiality when a diocesan bishop,
who does not himself accept the ordination of women to the
priesthood, but does not make any of the declarations in
clause 2 of the Measure, thereby does not prevent a woman
being ordained and licensed by another bishop to minister as
[a] priest in his diocese. Similarly, it will be a mark of continuing communion when a diocesan bishop in favour of the
ordination of women to the priesthood invites a bishop who
does not accept it to minister to priests and congregations in
his diocese who themselves do not accept it. In both cases
oversight remains ultimately with the diocesan bishop, who
remains the focus of unity in his diocese even when he
chooses to extend his oversight through another bishop. Such

extension should be seen as an expression of the collegiality of a House of Bishops which accepts the legitimacy of both positions.[5]

One of the overriding theological assumptions of the Act, illustrated very well by that passage, is the importance placed on the *collegiality* of the House of Bishops. One suspects that underlying this notion, at least at the intellectual level, are some borrowed clothes from the Roman Catholic Church where 'conciliarism' and the collegiality of the episcopal order represents the progressive and enlightened position compared to the monarchical papalism of the present pope. Conciliarism *is*, of course, the progressive stance in a Christian denomination in which the laity are excluded from participating in any formal institutional way in the *magisterium* and *imperium*, as they are in the Church of Rome. However, it represents a considerable retrograde step in a church, like the Church of England, which claims that it is 'episcopally led and synodically governed'. In the Church of England, the representatives of the laity constitute a formal 'house' of General Synod. We must remember that for all the emphasis given in Vatican II to listening to the 'sense of the faithful', it was never followed up by structural reforms that would have actually given the laity any formal power. One does not need to be a disciple of Foucault to see 'power issues' as important – being a disciple of Jesus will do. (Equally, of course, it is unthinkable that when women are ordained in the Roman Catholic Church that anything remotely resembling PEVs will be invented.) In short, the Act of Synod needs to be seen as the English House of Bishops' attempt to figure out just how they were all going to stay on reasonable terms with each other. Further, the elevation in the past few years of the rhetoric of 'collegiality' is a worrying sign in a church 'episcopally led and synodically governed'. The vast majority of the rest of the Church of England (i.e. every Anglican who is not a member of the House of Bishops) needs to ask whether the bishops' collegiality was bought at the expense of the *koinonia* of the rest of us.

Process

In Christian moral reasoning, the end does not justify the means and how things come into being deserves as much scrutiny as the substance. The contrast between the *process* of the Measure and the *process* of the Act is striking and raises crucial moral (never too strong a word when talking about 'power') considerations about the relationship between the layers of church government in which the laity and presbyterate participate and the growing oligarchical tendencies of the House of Bishops, which the Turnbull reforms will only enhance.

The 1992 Measure

Jean Mayland elsewhere in this book discusses the legislative history of the 1992 Measure in detail. Suffice it to say here that the Measure which General Synod and Parliament gave its final approval to in November 1992 and November 1993 respectively, was the fruit of a long, exhaustive (if not exhausting) and highly consultative legislative process which involved the most local layers of church government, begun in 1975.[6] It involved a series of drawn-out 'revision stages', as well as debate at deanery level. In 1990, 38 out of 44 diocesan synods agreed to the ordination of women. In November 1992, the Measure passed by a two-thirds majority in all three Houses of General Synod. A year later it progressed through Parliament (the voting figures in the Lords were 7:1 and 10:1 in the Commons). From March into the summer months of 1994, nearly 1500 women deacons were ordained to the priesthood, a number of whom had been in ordained or accredited ministry in the Church of England for decades. In 1988, Dr John Sentamu, now Bishop of Stepney, quoted his daughter Grace in a General Synod debate on the ordination of women: 'Well, let me tell you Dad, the Church of England, as far as I can see, has the power and engine of a lawnmower but the brakes of a juggernaut.'[7] It took twenty years to produce the 1992 Measure: let no one ever say that the ordination of women was a 'rush job'!

The 1993 Act

The same cannot be said for the Act of Synod. Considering the legislative history related above, the contrast in the evolution of the Measure and of the Act could not be more striking or telling.

1. In January 1993, the bishops issued their Manchester Statement, *Bonds of Peace*[8] and in April the Ecclesiastical Committee of Parliament started to meet to decide whether it was 'expedient' to send the Measure to Parliament. In June of the same year, the Bishops produced the Act of Synod which was not debated at the July meeting of Synod. The Act was aired for debate on the first day of the 1993 November Synod, sent back for revision, and voted on the *last day* of the same November meeting of Synod where it passed (one has to admit) by a very large majority.

2. The Act of Synod is an exclusive product of the House of Bishops, not of a synodical body with clergy and lay representation. That means of course, that it was produced by an entirely male and clerical body – not an insignificant factor.

3. The Act, in breath-taking contrast to the 1992 Measure, was never referred to diocesan and deanery synods for debate, reflection and *testing*. This accounts for the alarming ignorance among many usually well-informed laity and clergy about the content of the Act, because the more grassroots levels of our synodical system were not involved in the process of its passage.

Unquestionably the concept of women priests was far more rigorously tested through the body of the church than the concept of extended episcopal oversight. The latter reflects, surely, a more radical departure from a catholic understanding of orders than the extension of that order to include women. The Act, understandably given the speed with which it was manufactured, has all the hallmarks of a hastily constructed, unconsultative document. To put it bluntly: one must contrast nearly twenty years of testing and discernment of the ordination of women to the priesthood with ten months to produce the Act of Synod and to create the novelty of Provincial Episcopal Visitors. It is worth noting for future reference the speed at which that 'lawnmower' can move when certain interests are involved.

Theological reflection on the Act

To its architects and practitioners, the major arguments for the Act seem to be based on a certain understanding of the safe-guarding of consciences combined with a rather late conversion to the Anglican principle of comprehensiveness. First of all, what do PEVs have to do with the principle of Anglican com-prehensiveness? The Bishop of Richborough, one of the PEVs, wrote on this very point in response to criticism of the Welsh Church's decision to go down a somewhat similar road as the Church of England.

> Such an attempt at diversity in doctrine is no innovation. We have made comprehensiveness a virtue ever since the Elizabethan Settlement, for instance, managing to hold in one Church some who consider the Eucharist in a receptionist light, and so differ little from Zwingli, and others who believe in the real presence in a way indistinguishable from the Council of Trent. What is new, however, is the determination of the supporters of women's ordination to press ahead despite the very large minority in our Church opposed to this novelty.[9]

As a professional historian of the very period appealed to by the bishop, I must state that at no point in our history has the endorsement of comprehensiveness ever resulted in the creation of an extended or alternative episcopal system. Anglicans hold and have always held all sorts of views on all sorts of important doctrinal subjects, including issues as fundamental as whether salvation involves free will or is predestined. When has the

Church of England ever responded to this reality by anything remotely resembling the Act of Synod? The example of the eucharist the bishop uses is a good test case: if a parish priest and PCC do not share their bishop's understanding of the real presence, are they entitled to seek extended episcopal oversight? Surely not. Secondly, scholars of the sixteenth-century Reformation increasingly stress the unpopularity of the Reformation and that one cannot really speak of England as 'reformed' until well into Elizabeth's reign. The Elizabethan Settlement, which the bishop admires for its 'comprehensiveness', was an Act forced on the majority by a minority – perhaps there are some parallels there after all![10] Further, if the ordination of women Measure had failed to achieve a two-thirds majority in all three houses of Synod in 1992, I do not think we would be hearing much from the opponents of a priesthood 'comprehending' men and women about the virtues of 'comprehension': it is a principle which in application flows in only one direction. History teaches that Anglican comprehensiveness has endured precisely because diversity of belief and practice has not been contained by setting up competing or even parallel sacramental and episcopal structures.

A longer-term historical perspective provides an even sharper challenge and raises issues of far more fundamental theological concern than rather late in the day appeals to 'comprehensiveness'. One of the underlying theological principles of sacraments in the Western church was worked out in response to the Donatist controversies of the fourth century. The Donatists were a group of Christian rigorists who insisted that the orders and sacraments of anyone who had weakened in the face of fierce persecution were rendered invalid – or 'tainted' – by that action. The Donatists called such clergy *traditores*. These 'puritans' of late antiquity went so far as to reject the validity of the baptisms of persons conducted by such a *traditor* or who had been ordained by one – a type of negative apostolic succession. The Donatist controversy compelled Augustine of Hippo to take the Christian theology of sacraments and orders to a level of definition previously unknown in the church and his convictions have shaped all subsequent theological thinking on such matters. Ironically, Augustine is probably best known – and the most criticized across a range of Christian traditions – for his pessimistic view of human nature expounded in his battles in later life with Pelagius. Yet Augustine's insights into the nature of the sacraments and holy orders, forged by the bitter disputes with the Donatists, have continued to shape almost all subsequent theological thinking on such matters across the vast majority of churches. In a nutshell, the truly ecumenical, the truly *catholic* view we inherit from Augustine is that the individual qualities of a validly ordained minister or priest (or bishop), do not have any 'affect' on the authenticity of the sacraments administered by that individual. The Anglican expression of this doctrinal understanding is found in Article 26 of the Thirty-Nine Articles.

> Although in the visible Church the evil be ever mingled with the good, and sometimes the evil have chief authority in the Ministration of the Word and Sacraments, yet forasmuch as they do not the same in their own name, but in Christ's and do minister by his commission and authority, we may use their Ministry, both in hearing the Word of God, and in the receiving of the Sacraments. Neither is the effect of Christ's ordinance taken away by their wickedness, nor the grace of God's gifts diminished from such as by faith and rightly do receive the Sacraments ministered unto them; which be effectual, because of Christ's institution and promise, although they be ministered by evil men.

Powerfully, this is an understanding of ordination and sacraments which is upheld not only by the Roman Catholic and Anglican Churches, but by all the magisterial reformers of the sixteenth century as well. Freewill or predestination dogged the debates of the Reformation period, but even in those bitter times, this fundamental understanding of ordination and sacraments was upheld – until, one is tempted to say, the Act of Synod.

Is that too severe a criticism to offer? The Bishop of Ely in the November 1993 debate offered a strenuous defense of the validity of women's orders, while at the same time supporting the Act:

> When women are made priests in the Church of God by prayer and the laying on of hands, what will be done will be what the Church has always done since the days of the apostles.[11]

One is left with the question as to how one can hold that view *and* support the Act. To quote the Bishop of Richborough again:

> To enable us to coexist when Holy Orders were being altered has required that there should be places *where traditionalists could be sure of the valid orders of the celebrant* (my italics). So that this could happen, there had to be bishops to minister to these parishes and individuals.[12]

This is not directly a reference to the gender of the individual priest, but the implication is clear: there is doubt over the validity of the orders received from a bishop who has ordained women. Can such a view be described with any theological integrity as 'extended' episcopal oversight? 'Alternative' for all the denials, seems more precise. To rewrite Article 26 of the Thirty-Nine Articles, the unworthiness of the minister, does indeed hinder the effect of the sacrament. And in what sense can this view possibly be described as a catholic understanding of orders? The denial by members of the House of Bishops that a theology of taint underlies the invention of PEVs is deeply unconvincing. The Anglican House of Bishops is not a collective version of the papacy. In Anglicanism we assert that even Councils can err after all[13] and it is the duty of the defenders of the Act to produce *some* theological arguments from 'first principles' that will stand up to some intellectual scrutiny. The comparison is not a happy one between clergy in the fourth century who, under persecution, made offerings to idols, and a bishop who ordains a woman, or a male priest who works alongside an ordained woman colleague. Yet it is on this basis that extended episcopal oversight is applied: to avoid *physical* contact with bishops or male priests who have participated in the laying on of hands. It is hard to know what to call this except 'modern Donatism', a 'theology of taint'. Peter Brown's description of the Donatist mentality in his still magisterial biography of St Augustine of Hippo has striking resonances:

> Briefly, the Donatists thought of themselves as a group which existed to preserve and protect an alternative to the society around them. They felt their identity to be constantly threatened: first by persecution, later, by compromise. Innocence, ritual purity, meritorious suffering, predominate in their image of themselves. They were unique, 'pure': 'the Church of the righteous who are persecuted but do not persecute'.[14]

What the Act is *not* providing is protection for bishops opposed from being 'forced' to ordain women – those safe-guards are enshrined in the 1992 Measure. The Act is saying that if a bishop lays hands on a woman in ordination, others have the right to seek the ministry of a bishop whose hands have not been so exposed. (It is worth reflecting on how supporters of women priests denied themselves and were denied, any language about 'rights' in ordination. Supporters of PEVs, however, seem to see such provision as a 'right'.) The Act's supporters maintain that this is extended episcopal oversight, not alternative – that a PEV is really just another kind of suffragan. Quite remarkably, both *Bonds of Peace* and the Act itself are completely silent on the question as to why another bishop is doctrinally necessary under such circumstances. There is no theological rationale, no exposition of first principles, no 'theological seriousness' expressed as to *why* if a bishop ordains women he should not also come and conduct a confirmation in a parish over which he has the cure of souls. This 'real absence' is pretty staggering. More informally, the bishops publicly deny that there is any 'theology of taint' at work here – or a late-twentieth-century version of Donatism. Nonetheless, one must conclude that under attack in the Act is the fundamental catholic principle of ordination forged in the bitter Donatist controversies, upheld by the magisterial sixteenth-century reformers and expressed in the Thirty-Nine Articles as 'the unworthiness of the minister which hinders not the effect of the Sacrament'. Your bishop can deny the resurrection, the Trinity, and the incarnation; he may be a racist, liar, or thief – but no one will offer you a PEV. But if he ordains a woman to the priesthood, you can call in a 'safe pair of hands'.

Finally, let us for the sake of argument say that women really do not matter as much as men; that living with such a theology of taint is an acceptable price to pay. Let us forget half the human race and more than half the membership of the Church of England altogether and return to the issue of the protection of conscience and the Act.

In November 1996, the *Church Times* ran an article by a leading member of the ultra-conservative evangelical group Reform, David Holloway. Plainly and clearly, using the reasoning of the Act of Synod (and the Eames Commission), Mr Holloway laid out Reform's plans for their own Flying Bishops who would be 'sound' on the issue of human sexuality. The stance taken by the House of Bishops in the discussion document *Issues in Human Sexuality* is rejected by Mr Holloway.[15] In his proposal bishops will be required to sign a three-point document asserting their complete compliance with the belief that sexual activity of any kind (heterosexual included) by lay people and clergy, outside marriage, should be subject to 'appropriate discipline' in the church. A diocesan or suffragan bishop who refuses to sign this declaration will be forbidden pastoral and sacramental access to parishes over which he has, of course, the cure of souls.

> PCCs may then request their incumbent to invite for confirmations only subscribing bishops. This is not judgmental; it is saying that a failure to subscribe is indicative of impaired

koinonia. Once a bishop can subscribe to these points, *koinonia* will be repaired. The bishop is not banned – that is juridical and *ultra vires*. Rather it is a matter of invitation and welcome. Any subsequent non-diocesan confirmation would be valid, although irregular.[16]

Such a policy – if applied equitably – would dry up weddings in the Church of England to a trickle, but this is not the place to address Reform's particular point, but use it to illustrate the more important general point about church order and the protection of conscience. On what grounds, given the precedent created by the Act, is Reform to be denied? On what grounds is any group to be denied 'a bishop of choice' on any range of issues about which Anglicans of conscience disagree? Suppose one has different views from one's bishop on the remarriage of divorced persons, or the use of force in conflict – both important moral questions – may one have a PEV who has the same view? Why only on the issue of gender do we overthrow the time-tested doctrine that 'the unworthiness of the minister hinders not the effect of the sacrament'? A recent consultation at St George's, Windsor, which endorsed the state of play with the Act, did not adequately address this point:

> There was also considerable concern lest the Act of Synod be seen as a precedent for providing extended episcopal over-sight for other groups claiming that they could not, in con-science, receive the total ministry of their diocesan bishop. It was generally thought that a bishop's sacramental acts (i.e. ordination) has a *greater degree of objectivity and finality than a bishop's opinions on ethical or doctrinal issues* (my italics).[17]

This seems to miss the point entirely: it is precisely because a bishop's sacramental acts like ordination have 'a greater degree of objectivity and finality than a bishop's opinions' that the Act is so theologically defective. In November 1997, the Archbishop of York issued a stern rebuke to Mr Holloway's attempts to remove his parish in Jesmond from the jurisdiction of the new Bishop of Newcastle. Had Dr Hope not done so, he would have given in to a highly defective understanding of the relationship of conscience to the catholic orders of the church. However, one is left with the burning question as to what the qualitative difference is between what the vicar of Jesmond wanted and the provision of PEVs for the opponents of the ordination of women. Could it be that some consciences are more privileged than others?

Conclusion

We need to decouple the notion of a secure place for the opponents of the ordination of women from the Act. Many provisions were made for them in the 1992 Measure – provisions that were widely exposed to the scrutiny of the larger church. We need to decouple the Act from the principle of comprehensiveness – since for no other issue, even ones as much a matter of conscience as the ordination of women, is provision of this kind made. If the ordination of women is still in 'reception', then surely Flying Bishops are too. They are as much subject to scrutiny as anybody else. The Act creates a precedent profoundly undermining to our identity as an episcopal church, of catholic orders, and impairs our integrity when in ecumenical dialogue with other churches, both episcopal and 'non-episcopal'. The result of some 'theological seriousness' applied to the Act of Synod leads to the conclusion that to oppose the Act is the properly ecumenical and catholic position, and represents the true understanding of Anglican comprehensiveness.

4

An Act of Betrayal

I made my first speech in Church House on the issue of women's
ordination in a debate on the Women and Holy Orders Report
(1966) in July 1967. I made my last speech in 1989 in the debate
which led to the General Synod giving provisional approval to
the legislation to ordain women as priests. In 1990, the year I
left Synod, the Measure was referred to the dioceses. It received
final approval in General Synod in 1992 and the Royal Assent
in 1994. I was in Church House when the crucial debate took
place in November 1992.

Thus I had heard Church Assembly and General Synod
debate the ordination of women to the priesthood many times.
Successive bishops – Oxford, Birmingham, Southwark and
finally the Bishop of Guildford – moved motions in favour. We
received Commission Reports, House of Bishops' Reports, and
carefully balanced reports prepared by Christian Howard. We
debated the theology, the practicalities, and the ecumenical
aspects of the ordination of women over and over again. There
were debates in General Synod, diocesan synods, deanery
synods and PCCs. There were discussion in parishes and at
conferences. There were papers and books published, and
MOW carried out a whole educational programme. There were
letters from leaders of other churches both for and against and
there were comments from women ministers in other denomi-
nations. At the same time there were parallel debates about
women in the diaconate and women lawfully ordained abroad.

No one could deny that the subject was debated exhaustively
until there could be little left to say. It seemed to me that as the

years passed the debate continued with increasing theological depth and increasing passion. Looking back over the decades of the debates, I would sum them up by saying that in the 1960s no one really thought that the ordination of women would happen for many years; in the 1970s the debate became more serious and more theological and in the 1980s the opposition began to think that it might really happen and started to put effort into protecting their position. In the 1990s the legislation went through General Synod; the House of Bishops, worried by the outbursts of pain and rage, introduced the Act of Synod as an afterthought which, in my view, turned out to be ill-judged and divisive.

In 1975 the motion: 'that this Synod considers that there are no fundamental objections to the ordination of women to the priesthood' was carried by all three Houses of General Synod. A second motion 'that this Synod considers that the Church of England should now proceed to remove the legal and other barriers to the ordination of women' was rejected by the Synod because of the divided nature of the voting in diocesan synods. The Synod also voted on the motion: 'that this Synod, in view of the significant divisions of opinion reflected in the diocesan voting, considers that it would not be right at present to remove the legal and other barriers to the ordination of women'. This motion was defeated in the House of Laity. Other motions came and went.

In November 1984 a motion urging the drawing up of legislation came to the Synod by way of diocesan synod motions: 'that this Synod calls the Standing Committee to bring forward legislation to permit the ordination of women to the priesthood in the Provinces of Canterbury and York'. This motion, moved by the Bishop of Southwark, was passed in all three Houses.

In the debate the Archbishop of York, John Habgood, who spoke in favour, said:

the problem as I see it is how to persuade the whole Church to accept gladly and willingly that it is not maleness nor femaleness but humanity which is redeemed in Christ and that we remain impoverished unless humanity in both its genders can represent him in ministry.

The Archbishop also said that the matter must be taken slowly:

> I shall myself urge the Standing Committee to take things slowly, not as part of a foot dragging excercise but to allow new conversations to take place both between our churches, and within our churches, in the light of the new situation caused by our preliminary decision.[1]

On another occasion the Archbishop made it clear that if the legislation was passed, then all who were to be ordained in future must accept the decision and all new bishops must be prepared to ordain women, although he also said that the consciences of those in post must be respected. I believe that the Archbishop thought that if events moved slowly and people had time to think and to come round we would be able to move forward without division. Instead, of course, the slow procedure gave the opposition time to strengthen their cause and to make plans to safeguard their position if this 'thing' they dreaded so much really happened and women were ordained.

In July 1986 the General Synod debated a report by the Standing Committee entitled 'The Ordination of Women to the Priesthood: The Scope of the Legislation'. This report, produced by a group chaired by David McClean, set forward a number of possible options and ways forward. Professor McClean brought the report to the Synod on behalf of the Standing Committee so that the Synod could express its view on the four possible ways forward which it suggested. In his opening speech Professor McClean made it clear that he was outlining possibilities, not making proposals.

One possibility was a safeguard which according to Professor McClean would

> enable bishops, incumbents and parishes to maintain each in their own sphere, the discrimination on grounds of gender

which, in principle, the legislation would prohibit. This protects the conscience of those individuals though of course, at a cost to others.

The report distinguished between incumbents and bishops. Professor McClean commented that

Some will want to argue that it is right to protect the consciences of individual bishops but not to the extent of creating 'no go' dioceses. That view would involve bishops being required to delegate the duties that they felt unable to carry out personally . . . Another issue here is whether safeguards should extend to future bishops as well as to those already in office.

He himself favoured a simple opting out for parishes and limited safeguards for bishops which would prevent 'no go' dioceses.

The third option was one that filled Professor McClean with horror. It rested on a particular view on a question of sacramental theology which was set out in paragraph 33 of the report. According to this a bishop who ordains a woman renders his sacramental ministry invalid from that moment onwards. He cannot validly celebrate the eucharist; he cannot confirm; he cannot confer holy orders on men, let alone on women. On this Professor Mclean commented

My own position is that I cannot accept that any part of a Church can be allowed to repudiate a bishop who has acted in complete conformity with the official teaching and canon law of that Church . . .

One is led inevitably to the creation of distinct lines of episcopal succession within the Church of England; but that is extraordinary ecclesiology. A single Church cannot, surely, contain within itself two groups of bishops, the one not in communion with the other. Again I make no attempt to conceal my personal view; the proposition that a Church in that situation somehow vindicates a Catholic understanding of Church order seems to me a manifest absurdity.

The fourth option suggested creating two separate churches, by way of an officially approved schism in the Church of England. Professor McClean had little time for that and believed no one else had.

In the debate that followed many people expressed horror at the kind of scenario envisaged and stressed the need for the church to hold together. When Professor McClean came to the point of moving options for the legislation the Archbishop of York intervened to move that

> further consideration of this Report be postponed to enable the House of Bishops to report to the Synod before steps were taken to prepare legislation, the Bishops' Report to be presented not later than February 1987.

Clearly the bishops were very shaken by the kind of safeguards which were being demanded and the effects on their position. The Archbishop admitted that

> there was some horror in the House of Bishops when we found ourselves faced with a selection of recommendations, all of which, either directly or indirectly, affected our own ministry as bishops.

In supporting the Archbishop of York the Dean of Rochester (John Arnold) commented:

> When I read paragraphs 32 and 36, for the first time . . . literally could not believe what I was reading. I looked in vain for quotation marks and a footnote giving the author's name as Lewis Carroll, because I felt that I had gone through a looking glass to a world where values were turned upside down, perspectives reversed and a sense of proportion vanished. These proposals go clean contrary to everything about

the episcopal ordering of the Church which we have been urging upon other Churches in unity negotiations. We would certainly not tolerate them in our relationships internally.

I hope that the bishops will turn a resolute and united face against the notion that parishes could choose to go out of communion with them in this way.[2]

In February 1987 the House of Bishops duly presented a report to General Synod setting out the principles on which legislation should be based (*The Ordination of Women to the Priesthood*, GS 764). The Synod welcomed this unanimous report and passed motions which instructed the Standing Committee of the Synod to bring forward legislation to authorize the ordination of women and instructed the House of Bishops to prepare the Code of Practice envisaged in the report.

The Standing Commitee prepared a draft Measure for the ordination of women to the priesthood with safeguards for those who were opposed. They also proposed a Measure to make financial provision for those who felt obliged to resign if the Measure was passed.

In July 1988 the General Synod generally approved these drafts which were sent to Revision Committees for detailed consideration.

In May 1988 the bishops produced a theological report on the issues and in July 1989 their draft code of practice.

The kind of safeguards which were set out in the Measure were ones which gave parishes the right not to have women priests either as incumbents or curates or even to take occasional services. They also gave bishops the right to make a declaration that they would not ordain women. If they made such a declaration, their suffragans could not ordain either. Bishops could also declare that women ordained elswhere could not be licensed in their diocese.

Many of us who longed for the ordination of women were far from happy with this discriminatory legislation; we would have preferred a one clause Measure. We tried, however, to be charitable and supported these conscience clauses in order to show compassion and preserve unity. In order to reduce 'no go' dioceses and respect the consciences of bishops I sent in an amendment 'that a bishop should be allowed to make a declaration on grounds of conscience that he would not ordain women to the priesthood, but that this should leave complete freedom of action to a suffragan to whom the diocesan's function had been delegated'. This amendment was rejected on the grounds that 'a suffragan acted as the bishop's commissary and it was difficult to see how functions concerning women priests could be delegated to the suffragan when the diocesan was not in sympathy with the legislation . . .' and also 'because of the importance of maintaining the collegiality of the bishops within a diocese'.[3]

It is quite fascinating to note that in the Code of Practice to the Measure which was eventually put forward by the bishops they dealt with it by saying that a bishop who was not prepared to ordain women himself but was prepared to let other bishops do so should not make the declaration. He still need not ordain women but he could then let other bishops do so. This seems to me to be a example of casuistry and to be doing in fact what I had been told was in principle impossible!

Slowly the Measure dragged its way through the Revision Committee and in November 1989 came back to the General Synod for the next stage of approval. Many more amendments were moved and the debate was long and gruelling. In the end the process was completed and the Draft Measure as amended, together with the two draft Canons associated with it, was referred by the General Synod for consideration by the diocesan synods. As I walked back from General Synod to the house where I was staying, I saw newspaper placards and pictures celebrating the breaching of the Berlin Wall and showing people dancing on top of it. I felt that we had made a breach in the wall of partition which divided women from men and which centuries before St Paul had believed was breached through baptism.

In November 1992 the Measure came back to General Synod,

having been approved by a huge majority of diocesan synods. After a nail-biting debate it received the necessary majorities in all three Houses and was thus finally approved. In Dean's Yard this decision was met with tears and embraces and a whoop of pure joy which sent the starlings whirling. The deeply thankful song of *Jubilate Deo* went on and on and on. According to custom the Synod did not applaud and in the TV studio of Church House I pleaded with the Principal of Pusey House and his friends to stay within the Church of England. I was not prepared for what followed nor for the cost of apparent unity.

I had my first inkling of the situation at the Archbishop of York's Council Meeting at Bishopthorpe a few Saturdays later. The morning session was to be devoted to the discussion of the effects of the General Synod vote. With George Austin as the Archdeacon of York, I thought it might be quite a tricky session, but in no way was I prepared for the general atmosphere of doom and gloom and depression which prevailed. One might have thought that some terrible tragedy had taken place, or that the Church of England had voted for heresy, apostasy and schism all in one and had been thrown out of the Anglican Communion or the WCC.

There were long speeches about the pain of those who were opposed, the desperate situation of the Church of England, the fear of mass defections and the threat that numerous parishes would not now pay their quota. I couldn't help grinning when the Chairman of the Diocesan Board of Finance, who himself had consistently voted against the ordination of women, said very fairly that he would be more worried about the threat from a certain parish in Hull if it ever had paid its quota! It was about the one balanced remark I heard from any of the men present. Even those who had supported the ordination of women in the past seemed to be regretting their action and implying that they wished women would crawl back into the woodwork and stay there.

The Archbishop gave me two chances to speak. The one other woman on the Archbishop's Council did not say anything. In response to the general picture of doom and gloom, I said that

I thought that the vote was a wonderful sign of hope and new possibilities, not just for women, but for the whole church and for society. When one of the rural deans present said that we must meet in penitence for what had happened at the foot of the cross, I commented that we women and our supporters felt that we had been in the Garden of Gethsemane and at the foot of the cross for rather a long time and we now felt that we were in the Garden of Resurrection.

The mood of gloom, however, prevailed and went on prevailing. I actually do not think the opposition had expected the vote to go through and neither had the House of Bishops. They were not at all prepared for it, and did not know how to handle it. We women had developed our spirituality of waiting and grieving and hoping and trusting over many years. The opposition did not seem to have any spiritual depth with which to cope with the situation. The result was a scream of pain which the bishops could not tolerate.

The Archbishop of York had long supported the ordination of women intellectually and had made many helpful speeches, some of which I have quoted. I am never quite sure how far his heart was with us. The scream of pain caused his heart to be with the opposition but with all due respect I feel that on this occasion he lost his head.

Added to the misery and threats of the opposition came the rumblings of the Ecclesiastical Committee. This is the body in Parliament which handles the Measures which are passed by the General Synod and recommends to Parliament what action should be taken. It has the power to recommend that measures are not expedient and as they are often debated in Parliament at unsocial hours the Committee has considerable sway. Those opposed to the ordination of women had some good friends on the Ecclesiastical Committee which in 1989 had caused the defeat of a Measure to allow the ordination of a person remarried after divorce. The bishops were afraid of another defeat, although personally I think that there was a lot of bluff here for, as events showed, there was an enormous majority for this Measure in Parliament.

Anyway, the combination of the pain of the opposition and the threats of the Ecclesiastical Committee had a profound effect on the House of Bishops. At their meeting in January 1993 in Manchester, they agreed not only a Code of Practice but also the draft of an 'Episcopal Ministry Act of Synod' which made provision for parishes to petition their bishop to provide for someone other than himself to carry out appropriate episcopal duties in the parish. These duties should be carried out by a bishop who had not ordained women and if such a diocesan or suffragan bishop was not available, then the Archbishops should arrange for the consecration of additional suffragan bishops to 'act as provincial episcopal visitors'. The reports of the bishops' meeting described how they had greeted this agreement with joy and sang the *Te Deum* at the result.

I was shocked by all this. It went far beyond the limits of charity into deep, dark and dangerous waters. I objected for three reasons.

1. It was an act of betrayal of women by 'an old boys' network – a betrayal which demonstrated once more that women are expendable. The joy over the vote in General Synod in 1992 was not just joy over the priesting of women, it was joy because it seemed at last that here might be a sense that men and women, made in God's image, might be a true communiy of equals, and that the priesthood of creation given them by God might be reflected in the sacramental priesthood. The action of the bishops betrayed this hope. The Archbishop of York seemed to have given up his earlier hope, which I have already quoted, that the church might 'accept gladly and willingly that it is not maleness nor femaleness but humanity which is redeemed in Christ and that we remain impoverished unless humanity in both its genders can represent him in ministry'.

2. It was one thing to respect the consciences of clergy and parishes and not force women upon them, but it was quite another to allow them to choose to be ministered to, not by their own bishop but by one who had not ordained women. This was taking the whole argument into a completely different realm and seemed to me to be untheological, uncatholic,

unecclesiastical and completely contrary to the doctrine of the Church of England.

3. Far from assisting a process of reception, it seemed to me that this was a recipe for entrenching opposition and bigotry. It attempted to justify attitudes to women which were intolerable.

MOW was prepared to go along with the bishops' decisions, albeit reluctantly. I was not. I resolved to sign the petition against the Act of Synod and to attend the rally against it.

At the time I was working as Ecumenical Officer in the Diocese of Durham. I asked to see Bishop David Jenkins, both to discuss my attitude to the Act of Synod, and also to confer about some matters on the agenda of the diocesan synod. We spent a long time discussing the proposed Act of Synod. He took all I said about the 'old boys club', and the betrayal of women, but felt that because the diocesan bishop would voluntarily hand over pastoral care to an 'episcopal visitor', it would not break the unity of the church or become 'heretical'. When I challenged him as to why he had gone along with it he said that it was out of pastoral care for the opposition.

I wrestled very hard with this view and tried to go with it in a spirit of reconciliation, but just found it impossible. It was not that I wished to drive out the opposition and be hard hearted, but I was convinced that this approach was a terrible mistake. It was a kind but misguided afterthought on the part of the bishops which would have disastrous results.

I was no longer on General Synod, but if I had been I would have voted against the Act of Synod. Many people who did vote for it have said since how much they regret their action and what a mistake it was. Of General Synod members, only Philip Crowe and Bernice Broggio had the courage to speak out strongly against it. When one reads the account of the debate in General Synod it is clear that everyone was falling over backwards to be kind to those opposed, to meet their fears and needs. They dreaded being considered harsh, or strident, or uncaring.

The Act was introduced by the Archbishop of York who stated that:

It is an Act, a form of action, designed to ensure that the
Church of England remains the diverse and many sided body
that we have always known it to be. It is not a botched up
compromise to secure peace at any price. It springs from an
attempt to think through in a principled way how a Church
can remain united in the face of deep disagreement about
some aspects of its ministry . . . because the ordination of
women remains a contested matter both within the Church of
England and in the wider Church, proper space must be
allowed for those who doubt whether the decision was wise
or timely . . . In order to make space for this process of
discernment to continue and for a proper diversity to be
maintained, the House of Bishops has put forward arrangements to allow parishes and individuals, including bishops, to
distance themselves in varying degrees from actions about
which they have reasonable doubts . . . One of the important
safeguards lies in the role of the provincial episcopal visitors.
For this role their relationship with the two Archbishops as
titular suffragans in Canterbury and York is essential. My
personal hope is that they will not rush round conducting
services, here, there and everywhere – and I would at this
moment like to protest about the silly phrase 'flying bishops'
which is a journalistic gimmick that I hope we shall not use,
because it quite misrepresents what they are supposed to be
about. My hope is that they will act more as friends and
advisers for clergy and parishes, in a position to bring their
concerns to diocesan bishops and, if things have gone badly
wrong somewhere, to call on their archbishop to help. There
is no avoiding the pain of some degree of separation; but the
bishops are determined that the unity of the clergy with their
bishop, though it may be strained, will not be broken . . . By
enabling bishops to minister across diocesan boundaries on
behalf of one another, it underlines the collegial unity of
the bishops and points to a more complex understanding of
unity than that which is simply centred on the individual
bishop.[4]

This speech by the Archbishop of York obviously influenced people very strongly and the Act of Synod was passed after what was a very short debate held on one occasion, compared with the years of debate on the ordination of women. What he never explained was exactly why parishes and clergy would need a bishop other than their own and why their own bishop would not be accepted. He never even attempted to make clear on what basis episcopal visitors were necessary and justified.

I thoroughly support the desire to be charitable to those opposed to the ordination of women and have no wish whatsoever to drive them out. The fact remains that their consciences were well protected by the original Measure. No parish was obliged to receive women priests, no male priest was obliged to work with them, no bishop was obliged to ordain them. The clauses are clearly there.

In the Code of Practice to the Measure the bishops wisely made provision to remove the danger of 'no go' dioceses. They made provision for a diocesan who in good conscience felt unable to ordain women to provide for another bishop to do this.

What the Act of Synod did and does is something of an entirely different character. It is giving parishes freedom not to receive their own bishop simply because he has ordained women. This is not about charity or reception, it is about episcopacy, and the breaking of the bond between priest and bishop. The Code of Practice of the Measure says:

> Under section 7 of the Episcopal Ministry Act of Synod the Parochial Church Council of a parish where Resolution A or B is in force may petition the diocesan bishop concerned to the effect that appropriate episcopal duties in the parish should be carried out in accordance with the diocesan, regional or provincial arrangements described in the Act.

Resolutions A and B are based on the conscience clauses of the Measure, but this petition, which soon became Resolution C, is of an entirely different character.

In 1986 Professor McClean had said that

> My own position is that I cannot accept that any part of a
> Church can be allowed to repudiate a bishop who has acted
> in complete conformity with the official Canon Law of that
> Church . . . the proposition that a Church in that situation
> somehow vindicates a Catholic understanding of Church
> order seems to me a manifest absurdity.[5]

Yet this is exactly what the Act of Synod proposed. Parishes
were to be able to petition not to be ministered to by their own
bishop simply because he had chosen to do what canonically he
had power to do, namely to ordain women.

In the crucial 1993 General Synod Martin Flatman put his
finger on the anomaly. He announced that he was going to leave
the Church of England because of the vote to ordain women,
but made it clear that he would vote against the Act of Synod
because 'for the Church of England to legislate for some strange
kind of disunity within itself does not make sense to me'.

He went on:

> There are only two honourable positions to be in, certainly
> for someone from a Catholic tradition; either you are one
> with your bishop and his fellow bishops in working to pro-
> claim the gospel or you are not, and if you are not, well what
> do you do? . . . I feel an agony for those who cannot take the
> decision that I am taking, but I just say to them; if you are
> going to stay in the Church of England surely you have to be
> fully part of it? That is what being a Christian is about. If
> we are going to live in our little ghettoes, if we are going to
> legislate for some strange chequer board situation, I just do
> not, as a simple soul, understand what it is all about.[6]

The Dean of Rochester, John Arnold, who had once spoken
strongly against the idea of Provincial Episcopal Visitors, now,
as Dean of Durham, made an unhappy speech about them, but
like the huge majority who were swayed by the Archbishop of

York and desired to be magnanimous he voted for the Act. The Synod's collective heart ruled its collective head.

The style of PEVs has not developed in the way the Archbishop of York hoped it would. 'Flying bishops' have rushed around conducting services and fostering division instead of creating unity. In a recent article advocating the establishment of a free province Geoffrey Kirk, the Secretary of Forward in Faith, wrote:

> No one (not even, I suspect, former Archbishop of York John Habgood, the well meaning Frankenstein who brought it into being) expected, for example, that the three provincial episcopal visitors (PEVs, or 'flying bishops') appointed to care for traditionalists would have so extensive a role.[7]

Mr Kirk goes on to advocate the creation of an 'Autonomous Anglican Province' as the only way forward. To do that would take us further down the road of schism. This is to advocate the 'fourth option' set out in the Standing Committee Report to General Synod in July 1986 – an option which at the time Professor McClean said he had not time for and believed no one else had!

As things stand now, not only do parishes opt not to have their own bishops to confirm because they have laid their hands on women priests, they also refuse to have them into the parish to perform any sacramental acts. 'Flying bishops', on the other hand, are invited to celebrate and to preach. There are separate services for the renewal of vows on Maundy Thursday and separate services even for the ordination of deacons, even though the Code of Practice says this should not be so. The priesthood of women is described as invalid and eucharists celebrated by women are not recognized. In some places a theology of taint is peddled. Far from allowing a time of reception the provisions of the Act of Synod have entrenched opposition and divided the church.

On 7 October 1997 BBC Radio Four broadcast a 'File on Four' programme about the situation of women priests five years after the crucial vote in General Synod. Father Chris Collins and Father Beresford Skelton, two priests in the Diocese of Durham who are leading members of Forward in Faith in the diocese, were interviewed on the programme. In answer to a question both priests said that there was no doubt that their spiritual allegiances were to the Flying Bishop, the Bishop of Beverley, and not to the Bishop of Durham.

Father Collins said:

There's no doubt about that, the Bishop of Beverley is my bishop. He is the bishop that I pray for daily. He is the bishop that I look to for spiritual direction. He is the bishop that I look to as my Father in God.

When questioned about his attitude to the diocesan bishop, the Bishop of Durham, Father Collins said:

Whilst he is bishop, as I say, in juridical terms, I'm not actually in sacramental communion with him because of the action that he has taken over the issue of ordination of women and so I find it very difficult to even contemplate receiving communion at his hands . . .

When asked whether they would welcome their diocesan bishop to celebrate the eucharist in their parishes, Father Skelton replied:

No, he wouldn't be welcome – not for a eucharist. He would be welcome to attend non-eucharistic worship, but would not be allowed to celebrate at the altar . . .

This kind of statement is far more shocking to my Orthodox friends than the ordination of women. Roman Catholics say that such an Act would never be acceptable in their church. Lutheran women pastors (and other Lutherans) find it objectionable. Methodist women ministers are absolutely horrified by the Act and strongly oppose their church entering into unity talks with the Church of England while the Act remains in force. In June 1998 they moved a motion to this effect at the Methodist Conference.

The ordination of women to the priesthood came about after long years of debate and theological discussion and much prayer. The Church of England is greatly enriched by the gifts of women. Compassion has been shown to those opposed and their consciences are protected by the Measure. There is plenty of time for reception. The Act of Synod was an unfortunate and unnecessary afterthought by a House of Bishops excessively influenced by the pain of those opposed, and the threats of the Ecclesiastical Committee. In a mood of charity the General Synod unwisely passed the Act after a short debate. Many of those who voted in favour did so against their better judgment. The Act of Synod has developed in ways worse even than many of us feared. As it is so untheological, and doctrinally debate-able, and has proved itself to be divisive and ecumenically objectionable, it is high time that the House of Bishops reviewed its working with a view to recommending that it be rescinded as soon as possible.

5

Working the Act

PETER SELBY

The invitation to write for this volume did rather put me on the spot as someone who is working the Act. In writing this piece there is bound to be an element of self-justification and even defensiveness, and it is likely that it will seem that way even when that is not what I am intending. Rather than avoiding that issue, this piece is a personal one, a reflection on my own experience of watching the Act 'emerge' and then finding myself in the position of trying to work it.

'I am an extremist too'

Like many dioceses, Worcester has a grouping of clergy who do not accept the ordination of women, and like most bishops I have wanted to be in contact with them. I chose to approach the group on the basis that while our positions were in deep contradiction there was an element in my experience which paralleled theirs, the experience of doubting the integrity and authenticity of the ministry of the church in which I served. That referred in my case to the twenty-five years following my ordination in which women were not able to be ordained. While this was not an issue I had thought about constantly, it was always there in the background, forced to the surface whenever I had attended an ordination and especially when I presided at one.

This is by way of introducing myself as a person who thought of opening the priesthood to women not as an optional matter or a 'second order' issue, certainly not as something we should do because the time had come when the climate in the church and in society seemed to make it advisable, but as a matter of deep principle, touching on matters at the heart of the gospel. I had endeavoured, as a bishop in a church which did not ordain women, to put this into words in my book *BeLonging: Challenge to a Tribal Church*, and to set the issue out as one to do with the church's essential character as an *adoptive* community in which the freedom of God was the basis of its life and order, rather than those inherited or earned characteristics which are the basis of *tribal* or *ethnic* behaviour:

> For the question whether women should not now be ordained does not as a matter of fact present itself as an interesting idea that happens to have occurred to a few people. Nor does it emerge from the personal ambitions of a few women who think that they themselves should be ordained. It comes rather with the powerful energy of a generation that has recognised the patterns of behaviour that limit women's exercise of their gifts and is setting about dismantling them.
>
> More than that: it comes with the passion of a Christian generation that has recognised its vocation as God's adopted children to cease from the ethnic patterns of male dominance, and honour the freedom of God to call whom God chooses. That powerful energy and Christian passion of our time come together as a great longing for the valuing of all God's daughters and sons, their insights and their gifts.[1]

Of course there were elements in my experience which had provided a context for the development of that conviction and confirmation of it along the way: I had trained for the priesthood at an American seminary which had been the first in the Episcopal Church in the USA to admit married students and then, later, the first to admit women as students, even when it was not possible for them to be ordained. Later still, it had employed two of the women ordained at Philadelphia before it was canonical to do so. During my time as diocesan missioner in Newcastle, Jan, my wife, had accepted an invitation to be the diocesan contact person for the Anglican Group for the Ordination of Women, and with two other women had convened *NOW*, the Newcastle Ordination of Women group, which met regularly, mostly in our home. Those experiences, not to mention friendships and working relationships with a number of women who believed they were called to priesthood and whose colleagues, as well as those with experience of their discipleship and ministry, believed the same, strengthened my conviction on the matter.

But I believed then, and still believe, that those experiences were no more than context and confirmation, and that the movement to open the priesthood to women was grounded in a conviction about the freedom of God that was basic to the biblical witness and in accord with the gospel's central thrust. Because of that, I wrote in *BeLonging* some sharp criticisms of the way in which supporters of the campaign were presenting their case and of the compromises which they were willing to entertain. My strongest criticisms were reserved for the process itself, one in which those about whom the argument was raging had so little voice compared with those who opposed their ordination, and in which those who had made the implacability of their opposition clear still retained a strong voice in the detailed drafting of legislation they would in any case oppose. I characterized all this as *ethnic* behaviour, calculated to maintain the dominance of the male 'tribe' in the life of the church.

As well as the process, I found some of the features of the legislation deeply flawed. As the principal opposing speaker in the November 1992 Synod debate said, there is no logic about allowing women to be priests and not allowing them to be bishops; and I wholly agreed with the comment of an opponent friend about the financial provisions measure: 'The cost of conscience can be paid by me or for me; but it must not be paid *to* me.'

I moved from my post as a suffragan bishop to undertake a period of research in applied theology in the summer before the vote, aware of these flaws but still hopeful that at the vote the legislation would pass. I had perhaps been over-persuaded by friends who were convinced that what mattered was to get women ordained, and that after that people would be persuaded and the flaws rectified. My sense also was that whatever my reservations were, it was not for me to prevent the realization of this goal by opposing the compromises contained in the only legislation that was before us.

I travelled to London on the day of the vote, convinced that it would fail and that it was important for those of us who would be devastated by that, especially those whose ordination we were debating, to be together. There had been a number of other discussions in the previous months which had helped in the process of preparation for possible defeat, something I am firmly convinced opponents had not engaged in. When the Archbishop read out the figures I was amazed and over-whelmed; in the rejoicing that followed I lost my coach ticket home, but thought the price of a replacement money well spent!

A process of attrition

My own belief remains that the expectation of defeat on the part of many proponents, and indeed their preparation for that, meant that we were unprepared for the success of the vote and what would follow. Opponents would say that we had been warned by them many times; but I still believe, and said to those involved at the time on many occasions, that there followed a serious loss of nerve and clarity, and many decisions were taken while the institution was in some kind of corporate shock. I must however make clear, not least because of the title of this book, that those who were the principal architects of what became the Code of Practice and the Act of Synod had what they saw as very strong grounds for believing not only that some such settlement was right for the well being of the church as a whole but also that it was essential in order to secure the parliamentary passage of the legislation itself.

I was not part of the House of Bishops at that time, but I know from many who were that the members engaged in a good deal of soul-searching. When they believed that they had found a way to preserve the unity of the Church of England in the face of a deeply divisive issue they rejoiced together at what they experienced as an authentic gift of the Holy Spirit. I well see the power of that conviction; indeed I had written about it in the aftermath of the eucharist at Church House in 1986 when I had experienced a real struggle over the issue of collegiality and the idea of the bishops as the 'focus of unity'. I had concluded: 'Bishops do focus the Church, but they focus the Church as it is. Being a focus of disunity is not therefore in itself a sign of pastoral failure.'[2] I devoted a chapter of *BeLonging* to this very difficult area,[3] and believe even more in the light of the experience of the Act of Synod that the ideals of collegiality and of bishops as 'the focus of unity' need much more questioning than they generally receive at times of severe controversy, times at which they could be as much temptation as resource.

In any event, the view that the rights of opponents needed further safeguards gained influential support in the Ecclesiastical Committee and appeared to open up the possibility that the legislation would come to Parliament with a negative recommendation, with the risk that it would fail. It is not necessary to agree with any of those views to see their persuasiveness or to sympathize with those who saw themselves as having to make difficult judgments about what would produce the best way forward. Those of us who supported the legislation were not as a matter of fact continuing to sustain ourselves as a powerful movement with a well thought out programme or strategy, and if we now wish to say that the Act of Synod is seriously flawed the responsibility for that is one we share.

The processes that eventually yielded up the passage of the legislation and the passage of the Act of Synod did amount to a further attrition of the clarity in the legislation itself (and as I have said already that was in itself a somewhat defective clarity). I have always said that the Act of Synod is not, for reasons I shall state, something for which I could ever have voted – but when we make such statements we need to be aware that we were not at the time among those who had the responsibility of voting! As a movement we were opposed to the Act;

but we were never able to come together to issue an authoritative call to the effect that if it really were a choice between the failure of the legislation and voting for the Act of Synod we should wish to accept the former, however reluctantly. In the absence of such a call, supporters of the legislation in the Synod were left to make up their own individual minds; and the rest, as they say, is history.

A 'tribal' Act

The theological basis of my support for the ordination of women and of my objection to the Act of Synod are the same. I hold that the universe is created and sustained by a God whose loving will and purpose it is that human beings should engage creatively with each other. They do so as part of a created order which likewise discovers its own unity in a shared existence in which difficulties and quarrels, dilemmas and tensions are stayed with until their resolution emerges. Furthermore, the vocation of humankind is to accept, for all its difficulty, the inclusiveness of God's mercy and the need to relate to those persons, ideas and events which appear to us to go against our earlier experiences or otherwise present us with unwelcome challenges.

That view needs, of course, more explication than can be appropriately included here: not all new ideas are fruitful, let alone to be accepted. We have to own that the behaviour of some people may need to be resisted and their exclusion contemplated and even effected, because they represent a threat to the common life or our common apprehension of God's purpose so profound that it cannot be accommodated. You do not have to accept the too frequent application of the adage that 'you have to draw the line somewhere' to recognize its truth in the last resort.

Nonetheless, the acceptance of God's ever more inclusive mercy, of God's justification of us by grace alone, is the gospel's utterly critical challenge, revealed and enabled by Jesus Christ's life, death and resurrection. One of the key ways in which that is expressed is in the emergence of a community of faith in which membership is conferred by baptism, a membership which an individual can repudiate but which cannot be ended. Within the catholic order of the church, to which the Church of England subscribes, that fundamental communion we have with each other is further signified in our communion with the bishop. That communion may be broken through the divisions within christendom; but to break it wilfully is a very serious matter precisely because it undermines that central gospel challenge which the bishop signifies: that it is the good pleasure of a merciful God that we should live in a fellowship which witnesses to God's ever inclusive mercy and not seek to substitute for that fellowship a false one based on our personal choices of those whom we find it easier to like, or find more like ourselves or more ready to agree with us.

It is of course evident that there are within the Church of England those who believe that it is the bishops who, in ordaining women to the priesthood, have made it impossible for them to remain in communion. However, as I indicated at the time, the Act of Synod suggested to me that the fundamental reasons for ordaining women in the first place had not been fully appropriated by its supporters; and that the role of the bishop as sign of inclusion in a fellowship given by God's mercy was being compromised. For now everyone has, even if only at the back of their mind, the knowledge that the bishop ministers as the result of the choices of clergy and congregations, and that if they wish to they can change their choice and be offered oversight by another. That remains true even with the insistence of the Act that the diocesan remains the one with jurisdiction, for what is now *à choix* is the bishop's pastoral and sacramental ministry.

God's mercy now

In returning to work as a bishop I returned to work in the structures of a church in which the Act of Synod is in force. Even before I did so, I continued to be a bishop and was invited to participate in the ordination as bishop of the Provincial Episcopal Visitor for the northern province. I did so, and (paradoxical as it may seem) I did so for the same reasons as lay at the root of my opposition to the Act. What is more I saw it as my duty to offer such support and co-operation to him as I can, and likewise now work with his opposite number who has responsibility for the part of the southern province where I now serve, with as much graciousness and good humour as we can all muster. Their job as bishops is after all as demanding as that of any bishop and they live within considerable tensions, as will be obvious to everyone.

But more important than that is the simple fact that the church, despite the objections of many of us to the Act, has passed the Act and has appointed them to be bishops. That means that they have now become for me part of the way in which I am challenged by those very themes at the heart of the gospel which I have endeavoured to convey earlier in this chapter. The church may have (in my view) acted in a confusing way, may have given too much weight to pragmatic considerations, may have created a situation in which the episcopate no longer fully represents those deep and basic challenges; but the church I serve has acted in the way that it has, using the only decision-making processes it has, and has constituted the framework in which I undertake my episcopal task and in which I encounter the grace which has included me and challenges me to a ministry of inclusion.

In all of this it is too easy to write too much about the difficulties of opponents and the difficulties of those of us in positions of responsibility, in short as the Uppity Women so brilliantly said in one of their poems, 'to mention pain again'. It is important to keep hold of the fact (and it is easier to do this at some times than others!) that there have come to all of us the immensely exciting opportunities available to the church in appropriating the priestly vocation and gifts of women. That is more than enough to transcend all the confusions and muddles, however much energy they may consume. It is also crucial to make clear within the Church of England what the Act and the legislation were doing and what they were not: they were making provision for something new to happen and at the same time to respect the view that opposes that development *in conscience*. The legislation and the Act were not permission to be morally lazy. They are not there to enable us to support the ordination of women as long as it happens somewhere else. They are not there to provide an excuse for us not to take the steps necessary to support women in their ministry, nor do they exist in order to free us from the obligation to enable women to seek priestly work by building equal opportunities processes into all those situations not covered by the right of *conscientious* objection.

It may appear inconsistent to be saying at the same time that the provisions of the Act and for conscientious objection must be fully accepted, and to treat with respect, warmth and grace those who avail themselves of what they see as protections against a development which they do not accept, while at the same time making it clear to them that the priestly ministry of women is a development which as bishop I am charged to further. But both positions are grounded for me in the same fundamental gospel truth, and that means that if their fundamental consistency is unclear to us at the moment it must nevertheless become clear in the end.

That does not of course answer the question 'What should be our aim in any review of the Act's operation?' or even settle the issue raised by many whether it was simply a temporary expedient which can be expected to 'wither away' in due course. I am not in the business of foretelling the future, and it is not surprising that opponents of the ordination of women see the prediction of its 'withering away' as simply patronizing. Given the journey we have travelled I see no alternative to engaging together in the search for something better, something which respects conscientious objection and at the same time avoids offering people the opportunity to 'choose the bishop you agree with'. We also need a way of working that offers women some assurances about their having equal opportunities in appointments.

What kind of a solution that might be is not clear at the

moment. What is clear is that our present position is due precisely to that failure to wait with the anger and disappointment of those who felt the vote as a 'defeat' for long enough for the future to emerge with clarity. That suggests that we are at a point where neither campaigning for instant repeal nor sitting back and waiting for the Act to 'wither away' makes sense. We have to learn the meaning of where we have got to and how it happened, something I have sought to write about here, and to continue to work for more clarity in our thinking than has been shown hitherto. Meanwhile we work as hard as possible at the development of women's opportunities for ministry and to witness to the blessing that the ordination of women has brought.

Mercy and the church

At the end of this argument a central theological question is left in the air. It is about the status of the church when it appears full of compromise, limping between two opinions and when, as I have said, those entrusted with leadership within it have to speak words of both conviction and compromise at the same time. The reality of this is not new: in the consideration of all sorts of issues I have come again and again to reflect on the Council of Jerusalem, the first 'general synod' of which we have a record, and which also had to consider basic issues of inclusion in a situation which was throwing up contradictory convictions, powerful traditions and new experiences as it debated what was to be expected of Gentile converts. The 'act of synod' is there presented to us (Acts 15.23–29). We read it as the charter for an inclusive and universal faith. Any reading of that text, however, brings one up against the evidence of compromise and disputed interpretation, phrases of which the meaning is unclear, and above all the sense that we are here in the presence of searching for an agreement in which not all would get all they wanted. Whatever the precise order of events may have been, the New Testament suggests that compromise, disputed meaning, contested interpretation were the stuff out of which the universality of faith emerged as the inheritance into which we enter.

As it was in the beginning, is now and . . . ? If that is how the dynamic of divine mercy was active in the earliest days of the church, a dynamic that continued *despite* (or was it *through*? – that is surely the question) arguments that appeared unresolved and conclusions that appeared to leave much open to subsequent dispute, what does that say about what we may expect of the church? Certainly we should expect as much clarity as we can, and we should struggle for it; we should expect to achieve more clarity than we did over the ordination of women. That is a struggle that can and must continue. But we should also not burden ourselves with a perfectionist theology of the church, one that makes it the only institution that does not rest on God's continuing mercy to hold it in being. Because of that continuing mercy we should struggle for clarity in our pursuit of the truth and justice God requires; because of that mercy we may still have hope.

6

Where is the Catholicity?
A Methodist Looks at the Act

IAN JACKSON

I see the church as a community of women and men who, together, in and through their differences, express something of the variety and vitality of God. I take it as self-evident that God's definition of humanity as male and female in creation should be reflected in the way that human beings order the earthly institution of the church. I cannot see the exclusion of women from office or influence as anything other than a distortion of the gospel.

I have spent most of my ministry trying to make sense of the gospel with people who do not come from a church background and for whom traditional expressions of faith and traditional ways of ordering church life mean little. I have come to see faith through their eyes. I believe that there is yet more to learn; that the church is continuing to discover how to be more inclusive, how to be more open, and how to incorporate into its life the dynamics of a wonderfully diverse humanity. I am also a convinced ecumenical Christian.

The Act of Synod, therefore, represents, for me, a step backwards from inclusiveness, a drawing of a tighter circle which, as well as being an injustice to women, is profoundly unhelpful to those who look to the church to deepen their understanding of a humanity created and loved by God.

This is a *personal* Methodist perspective. Although I have sought opinions about the matters I discuss, my thinking is not necessarily representative of Methodism in general. It is shaped by my experience of ministry in stressed urban areas, working, by preference, with non-church people. Also of living and working with my wife, Chrissy Ross, who was involved in the early days of the Christian Feminist movement and the Movement for the Ordination of Women. My standpoint is skewed, shaped, enriched and fashioned by these facts, but I make no apology for it. It is the place where I stand.

The Methodist experience of women

Methodism has a long memory of women's ministry. Although hardly a proto feminist movement, early Methodism did release an enormous amount of female vitality. Marginalized because of gender, class and education, women touched by the Wesleyan revival found that their skills of encouragement, preaching and organization were nevertheless valued in the early years. The slightly anarchic dynamism typical of the first phase of so many religious movements meant that early Methodism was influenced by women's insights. The 'class system', in which people met to worship in informal settings, an organizational ploy in some ways, drew much from a domestic and emotional world where women were far more fluent and comfortable. Inevitably women fared badly in the aftermath of Wesley's death. Male hierarchies organized the new church to give it legitimacy and a recognizable place. Women didn't fit into this tidying up operation and the most significant continuations of women's ministries were not in the hierarchical Wesleyan Methodist system which limited women preachers in 1803 and finally banned them in 1835, but in the more turbulent Primitive and Bible Christian off-shoots. The Victorian era dealt with Methodist women in much the same way as it did with their sisters in other churches. The values of quiet domesticity, submission and interior piety were inculcated. They engaged in philanthropic endeavours and supported the increasingly professionalized male clergy. This female serving ministry was institutionalized in 1890 with the founding of the Wesleyan Order of Deaconesses.

The principle of women's presbyteral ministry was first accepted by Methodism in 1939 but it was not until 1974 that women were ordained as presbyters.

Methodism officially stands foursquare behind this democratic decision. It continues to make clear that women are an irreversible and non-negotiable part of its ministry. Although British Methodism has not retained or adopted a threefold order of ministry, those who chair Districts are rightly seen and acknowledged as being the equivalent of Anglican bishops. These positions are open to, and have been occupied by, women. There is, of course, still some sense in which women are not represented at all levels of church life. In the 1986 response to the ecumenical report *Not Strangers but Pilgrims*, the Methodist Church said that 'Women play a major part in the life of the Methodist Church, frequently in positions of responsibility in the local church and circuit, less often at district or regional level, or in the committees of the church.' In the report *The ministry of the people of God*, adopted by the 1986 Conference, the point was made that 'Women have been ordained by the Methodist Church since 1974, but there has been little discussion of how our understanding and practice of ordained ministry should be influenced by our experience of the ordained constituting a community of women and men.' Nearly ten years later not much seemed to have changed. The 1995 report to Methodist Conference, *Called to love and praise: the nature of the Christian church in Methodist experience and practice*, noted that 'Methodism . . . fully endorses the equality of women and men in ministry, whilst recognizing that the distinctive contribution of women's ministry to the wholeness of the Church has yet to be fully explored and realized.' Kathleen Richardson, the first and, as yet, only woman President of Conference, in her Presidential address of 1992 commented that it was 'twenty years since the Methodist Church expressed its consent to the ordination of women. Today some 9% of our presbyters are women and the influence and significance of that decision is, I believe, beginning to make a difference as to how we perceive and conduct our life together as a community of women and men, in the church and in society. But it is not without pain, as many women will testify, and there are still areas of our church life where the ministry of women needs to be more strongly affirmed.'[1]

These comments were borne out by the way that the 1995 report *A Cry of the Beloved*[2] was produced and received. Commissioned to reflect on twenty years of experience of women as presbyters, the report painted a bleak picture of the way that women were treated by the church. The report spoke of the hurt of women who were marginalized by male colleagues, frozen out of decision-making, neglected by those appointing senior positions and barely tolerated by circuits who could not wait to return to a real, male ministry when they departed. It pointed to the disproportionately low number of women superintendent ministers and to the way in which the ordination of women had failed to catalyze a broader reassessment of theological language, church power structures, or ecclesiastical style. It recognized that this was not only the experience of women – men, also, were victims of patriarchal and hierarchical models of ministry, in having disappointing experiences of working in the church. It made it clear that not all women shared these feelings or analysis but, nevertheless, thought that these experiences were serious enough for the church to adopt a series of measures which would monitor the treatment of women by the church. The report recommended that Methodism used a set of equal opportunities measures to get a true feel for the situation. Conference debated the report in the session before lunch, notorious in that attention is usually elsewhere. A succession of women who did not recognize their positive experience in the report urged caution and Conference did not respond well to what it clearly saw as an over emotional and unbalanced report from a group of malcontents. The report was received rather than adopted – a polite way of saying 'No thank you'. However Methodism, ever pragmatic, did take note of the spirit of the report, and has made efforts to move towards proper monitoring of the position of women. The question is whether the changes are substantial. It is no coincidence that the succession of reports noted above, which talked either of the lack of women in leadership, or of the lack of learning by the church from women, were not accompanied by calls for positive action. It was as if Methodism expected the situation to change by itself – that time would alter our theology, our church order, our power bases. It seemed inevitable that it would be the women who had to bear the sufferings that went with these birthpangs of the new.

A look at the Act of Synod from a Methodist perspective

The very existence of something like the Act of Synod is un-natural to a Methodist mind.

There are at least three separate but linked issues at stake here about the nature of church order – the nature of its catholicity, its authority and the oneness of its ministry. Then there is an issue which relates to the nature of Christian charity. Finally there is an issue about the actual purpose of the church.

Catholicity

The decision to ordain women to the presbyterate in the Methodist church was not without opposition. However the catholic spirit of the Methodist Church was such that having voted for the measure it was inconceivable that the church as a whole would not adopt the practice. Methodists looked with amazement at the Church of England, which voted so over-whelmingly to affirm the principle of ordaining women to the presbyteral ministry and then turned itself inside out trying to mitigate the consequences of this for those who were so decisively outvoted. The introduction to the Code of Practice for the Priests (Ordination of Women) Measure 1993 says that 'Christian charity and the exercise of true pastoral care require that careful provision be made to respect as far as possible their [those opposed to the ordination of women] position . . .' This looks suspiciously like saying to white southern Africans that it would be just fine to continue to have a white Natal or a white

Rhodesia within countries ruled by black majorities. One of the proud boasts of the Church of England, one of the things it offered as gift to the wider church, was its ability to contain difference within one communion. But this new development seems like the maintenance of communion at the cost of an extraordinary sleight of mind. If this is what catholicity means to the Church of England it is not what it means to Methodists. It looks like a road towards separate development.

Authority

Authority within the Methodist church lies with Conference and is expressed through the notion of the connexion. The Methodist principle of connexionalism implies a networked and interdependent view of the church. The part is indivisible from the whole. The fullness of the expression of the church in a particular place is never an indication of its autonomy but of its focussing, and representing, the resources of the whole in the local. The independence of local churches in the variety of their cultural and social representations is not a breaking of fellowship with the whole but a contribution to the diversity that is the lifeblood of such a network. What connexionalism will not allow is the coexistence of competing versions of church order. It is inconceivable that within the one Methodist connexion there could be pockets of the church which officially declared themselves 'women-free zones'. For Methodism, a legalized 'two integrities' would mean an actual two churches. Since authority resides in Conference and not in individual bishops, there is no possibility of Methodist ministers seeking to find episcopal oversight that suits them, of placing themselves under a person who by their own authority and practice preserves a truer form of the church. This is further reinforced by Conference's power to station presbyters where it wishes. If women presbyters pollute the church, the Methodist connexional system is a most efficient way of spreading the contamination! The legislation enshrined in the Measure and enabled to be enacted by the Act of Synod seems to be a bizarre

combination of personal princely authority in the bishop and a
sort of unchallenged congregationalism. These two forces look,
to Methodist eyes, like the thin end of an anarchic wedge. Can
we really conceive of a church where congregations are free to
seek episcopal oversight to suit any particular set of prejudices
they may have? The experience of David Holloway's parish at
Jesmond, with its refusal to accept episcopal oversight from a
bishop who just might have expressed a modicum of sympathy
for lesbian and gay people, suggests that this is not too fanciful.
Perhaps we are moving towards a pick-and-mix church where
we can find just the right episcopal oversight for any particular
niche of needs.

Oneness of ministry

A third issue relates to the fundamental indivisibility of
ministry. British Methodists still rejoice in a presbyteral ministry
which is free from gradations of deacon, priest and bishop.
Although in ecumenical dialogue they have affirmed the possibility of seeing the threefold order as a possible expression of
unity, they would only move in this direction if proper emphasis
was laid on the ministry of the whole people of God and on the
importance of collegial and conciliar modes of church government. Calling to a specialized office, as for example, superintendent, Chair of a District, connexional secretary or
President of Conference, is seen as a call to a representative
ministry, not a ministry of a different ontological variety. Chairs
of Districts can, and do, move back to the life of circuit ministry
at the end of their term of office. Linked to this is the fundamental assertion that women and men are an equal part of this
indivisible ministry. Some of the provisions of the Measure, its
associated Code of Practice and the supplementary Act of Synod
are incomprehensible from this point of view. Most acutely –
how can it be possible to ordain women to the office of priest
but not bishop? What understanding of church order is in
operation? How can a church believe in the full access of the
priestly ministry of women while at the same time placing

obstacles in the way of a woman testing vocation? For example, the Code of Practice states that where a woman applies to have her vocation tested in respect of non-stipendiary ministry and has, because of the attitude of her own diocesan bishop, to go to a neighbouring diocese, 'A neighbouring bishop approached by a woman candidate for NSM ministry under this Code of Practice will have to consider the possibility of the candidate receiving a licence, which may depend upon her ability to move to his diocese.' Such a situation looks like plain sexual discrimination. Moreover the notion that a woman seeking refuge in a sympathetic diocese becomes, when sponsored by the diocesan bishop, the financial responsibility of that diocese, in respect of her training, is a strange idea for Methodists. Methodism tests vocation in a uniform way, shares the costs of training as a whole church and, through Conference, finds work, as itinerant ministers anywhere in the country, for all those, women and men, who have been tested and trained.

The idea that it is possible to ordain a man opposed to women's ministry to serve in a parish also opposed would be out of the question to Methodists, for whom ordination always happens at and by the authority of Conference. Ordinands are ordained together, to the one ministry. A privatizing of ordination would be, for Methodists, a denial of the unity of the one ministry. The continued acceptance of Anglican male ordinands who deny the possibility of women's ordination, and their continuing ordination in parish churches which also reject women, seems to legitimize those who want to continue to promulgate 'true faith' in an apostate church.

Methodists have had to wrestle with the implications of the indivisibility of their ministry in respect of women. Practice has taken, and is taking, a painfully long time to catch up with theory. Only at Conference of 1998 were Standing Orders introduced to make it illegal for a male minister to offer ministry in a case where the ministry of a woman had been rejected on the grounds of her gender. This position is entirely contrary to the position outlined in the Code of Practice regarding occasional offices where communion is combined with marriage or funeral services and where the House of Bishops 'expect(s) incumbents to respect the wishes of those concerned as to the gender of the president'. For Methodists the one ministry of the church is offered through each presbyter in full connexion with the Methodist conference. Placing as paramount the individual prejudices of people who want the ministry of a man but not a woman would imply an unacceptable fracturing of the one ministry.

Charity, courtesy and respect

The Code of Practice for the Measure and *de facto* for the supplementary Act of Synod ends on a typical upbeat note.

> The arrangements in the Priests (Ordination of Women) Measure and the Episcopal Ministry Act of Synod provide a framework within which those members of the Church of England of differing views on the ordination of women to the priesthood can seek to remain in the highest possible degree of communion with one another. Mutual respect and trust will be essential if all the arrangements are to work successfully. The aim must be for all to continue to participate in every aspect of the Church's life to the fullest extent which individual conscience will allow, showing at all times that charity, courtesy and respect for others which are among the hallmarks of the true Christian.

This is a well-known trick. When we saddle ourselves with indefensible, illogical and unworkable positions, the church frequently calls us to apply the meeker Christian virtues. The trick is usually applied to those who are the victims of these positions and is certainly a time-honoured tactic used by men to remind women of their place. When women point out that they are merely asking for what belongs to normal human dignity, or when they highlight the inconsistency of the positions called for by the Act of Synod they are accused of being out of love and charity, of rupturing fellowship. It is by no means a modern trick. Rowland Young wrote in 1880:

'Man is strong; woman is beautiful. Man is daring and confident; woman is diffident and unassuming. Man is great in action; woman in suffering. Man shines abroad; woman at home. Man talks to convince; woman to persuade. Man has a rugged heart, woman a soft and tender one. Man prevents misery, woman relieves it. Man has science, woman taste. Man has judgment, woman sensibility. Man is a being of justice, woman an angel of mercy. These comparative characteristics represent Man as the head, woman as the heart; or Man the intellect, Woman the affection. And in doing so we submit that no position derogatory to Woman is involved therein.'[3]

The trick is to assign women a subordinate place in the hierarchy of power whilst at the same time to elevate her virtue. It is a trick which some women also play and collude with. Frances Power Cobbe, a nineteenth-century women's campaigner, wrote: 'Here is the root of the misplacement of women, that they have been deemed by men, and have contentedly deemed themselves, to have only a secondary purpose in the order of things.'[4] What therefore is of crucial importance, what would be the best expression of charity, courtesy and respect is not to institutionalize prejudice but to work out what it means to be a church which is truly a community of women and men where none is misplaced but all could take their own rightful place, where all could come down 'where they ought to be'. It may be argued that this is an infringement of individual conscience, that it excludes those who oppose the ordination of women, who say 'In all good faith I cannot accept that women belong in the priesthood: it is not a matter of prejudice, but of what has been passed down from scripture and tradition, a practice which derives from the Lord himself. My conscience requires that I do not discard this deposit of faith, it is not a culturally determined extra, but a bedrock belief.' We should have the charity to take such people seriously and must do them the discourtesy of inviting them to a larger freedom and a wider respect.

What it means 'to be the church'

Working, as I do, with many people who don't go near the church and living in Greenwich where the millennium frenzy is most potent, it is perhaps not surprising that the questions 'What is the church for? What is faith? What does it mean to believe in God? What sort of church is required in the next century?' are questions that are addressed to me and that exercise me. Looked at from this liminal position, of people on the margins of the church at the threshold of a new millennium, the Act of Synod seems an irrelevance, a confirmation of low expectations, an offence and an excuse. An irrelevance because it appears to be the Byzantine solution to an arcane problem unrelated to the mass of ordinary people; a confirmation of low expectations, because what else can you expect from a church so out of touch with people; an offence, because it is so obviously discriminatory; and an excuse, because it continues to allow people to dismiss the claims of faith because of the state of disarray of the messenger.

A church which can produce such an Act of Synod is far removed from the only church that people would and should take seriously – a church which is inclusive, unfussy, related to immediate tangible concerns, uses concrete and vernacular language, is angry at, and critical of, injustice and incarnates a culture of equality and truthfulness. As Charles Gore declared in 1892, 'We must devote our energies to making the Church adequate to the divine intention, as strong in principle, as broad in compass, as loving in spirit, as our Lord intended her to be'[5]

Conversations between the Church of England and the Methodist Church

In November 1997 the General Synod agreed to hold formal talks with the Methodist Church about the issues raised in '*Commitment to Mission and Unity*, a report of the group of Anglicans and Methodists set the task of having informal talks about the desirability of talking! In June 1998 the Methodist

Conference also agreed to these talks. They will be wide-ranging, taking in many aspects of church life and addressing many shared concerns and divisive issues. Due to start in autumn 1998 they will face the most considerable difficulty over the question of women's ministry. '*Commitment to Mission and Unity*' recognizes this obstacle. In the section which asks 'Is this the right time for formal conversations?', the report states that

> no step ought to be taken which would threaten the degree of communion which exists in either of our churches. In both churches there are delicate balances to maintain on various issues. In particular, the Church of England, since it began to ordain women to the priesthood in 1994, has been involved in a process of discernment concerning this development in the ordering of the ministry of the universal church. This process is seen as continuing until all the churches reach a common mind. The Church of England has retained a space for those who are opposed to the ordination of women to the priesthood. They are assured an honoured place through the provision of episcopal oversight which supplements the diocesan system. We are agreed that any change in relation-ship between our two churches must honour this attempt at securing comprehensiveness and at living with differences during a process of discernment. Equally, though, we are agreed that the Methodist Church cannot contemplate limit-ing the ministry of oversight already exercised by women or excluding them from participating in the ordination of deacons and presbyters.[6]

Being a joint report, this rather understates the Methodist position. The ordination by the Methodist Church of women to the one ministry, which includes the ministry of oversight, is non-negotiable. Even though the talks may not be about organic union between the two churches they will take in issues of joint oversight. Church of England regulation and pro-nouncement explicitly excludes women from the episcopate. Methodists could not contemplate the deliberate exclusion of women from oversight. It is impossible to see how this really practical clash of ways of operating can be resolved. Methodism is not in a period of discernment about women's ministry any more than it is in a period of discernment about men's ministry. If anything, Methodists would see the talks as an encouragement to Anglican women and as a way that the Church of England might move beyond discernment to a positively joyful acceptance of women's presbyteral ministry and the speedy opening up of episcopal ministry to them.

For some Anglican women the decision of the Methodist Church to enter into formal talks with the Church of England is seen as an act of betrayal. 'How can you talk to a church which legalizes precisely the discrimination which, in your own life, you oppose?' Methodist answers range from an affirmation of this point of view, to a sad acknowledgment of the plank in our own eye over so many things, to the claim that because we are not talking organic union we can talk with a church whose ministry we do not recognize as complete, to the Trojan Horse approach outlined above – the talks will hasten Church of England development in this area.

The challenge to those talking is not to keep silence about what is most problematic. A willingness to address differences in approach to women's ministry would signal a desire to talk about fundamentals. A tenacity by the Methodist participants in keeping before their colleagues the gift to the church of the full acceptance of women's ministry would lend the talks a necessary missionary and ecumenical shape. Ecclesial conversations always run the risk of talking about trivia, of fiddling while Rome burns. By placing the acceptance of the full humanity of women at the centre of the agenda these talks could help to make the church both more attractive, more fully connected with people's lives and more truly representative of the whole household of God which is the inner dynamic of real ecumenism. The most unsatisfactory outcome would be some form of agreement in areas such as the threefold ministry, the nature of the diaconate, the relation of church and state and the understanding of church membership and confirmation, whilst leaving the question of women's ministry to be resolved at some later, indeterminate date.

Methodism has its roots in the Church of England as a radicalizing movement which engaged people who felt excluded from church life and which sought to reshape the church as a missionary body. It also confronted people with the need to make radical choices in this 'present age'.

When Methodist Conference debated whether or not to engage in the talks it also debated a parallel amendment which called on the church not to start talking until the Church of England had rescinded the Act of Synod. Although this amendment was not adopted it received considerable support. Those who represent the Methodist Church in the talks will take with them the clear view that the Act of Synod is untenable and unjust. It will need to be faced and dealt with swiftly to allow progress in the talks on other issues. This could then help to shape the whole course of the conversations. The talks could illustrate the truth that ecumenism is a twofold process of discernment and reformation. In it the church perceives and appropriates, ever more clearly and fully, the reality of the unity of creation and human beings, and, as a consequence, equips itself to be more responsive to the absolute inclusiveness of the gospel by the way it orders its life. This process is authentic when it extends justice to those who have been denied it, includes those who have been excluded and brings those without power into the centre.

The Act of Synod deprives women of equality of opportunity in the Church of England. It will hamper talks with the Methodist Church and is a denial of the full and free community of women and men which is the goal of the gospel. It must go.

7

At the Grassroots: The Act in the Parishes

LESLEY BENTLEY

I am a priest working in a parish as vicar, in the Diocese of Liverpool as Dean of Women's Ministry, and in the wider church as Chair of the Network of Diocesan Advisers in Women's Ministry. My context is a church that has now ordained around 2,000 women as priest since the first ordinations in 1994. At 31 December 1997 there were 622 women in incumbency status posts (including chaplains) and there is every reason to think that this figure is now much higher. In a recent survey of thirty-three dioceses, Deans of Women's Ministry were asked if any woman priest remained as a curate who could reasonably expect to be an incumbent now. Twenty-one reported that they had, at most, one women remaining unplaced. The clear picture is of a church in which women are integrating quickly to the priesthood. Stories that now circulate are less often the painful ones of rejection, although these are still around as the recent Manufacturing, Science and Finance Union report on harassment made clear. The newer stories tend to be more encouraging. There are positive reports such as, 'I met the local lay Chair of Forward in Faith at a eucharist in her own church, she hugged me, asked who I was, and upon discovering that I was a neighbouring incumbent, declared her role and hugged me again.' There are the puzzling ones: '. . . when I thought about the churchwarden's query about the Easter flowers, I realized that he not only expected me to be the vicar, but also the vicar's wife.' There are those signifying how the issue is a non-event: '. . . gender just was not an issue with the parish representatives when they interviewed me about the post; they were all used to women in authority at work and could not see what the fuss was about.'

This picture is not uniform, of course; there are still areas where women report hostility, more often from clergy than from laity. Considering, however, that it is only four years since the first ordinations, it depicts a church in which women priests are already the norm in some areas and fast becoming so in others.

When I was ordained as priest in 1994 with twenty-seven other women in the Diocese of Liverpool, two of the clergy whom I knew to be opposed to the ordination wrote to me. We knew each other fairly well, as we had spoken against one another at several Parochial Church Council debates. Their sentiments expressed the paradox that they could not agree with what was happening, but they hoped that we would be able to continue to work together. One has since left the diocese (not as a result of this issue) and I work with the other on a regular basis as we maintain a network of Spiritual Directors in the diocese, and arrange for their training. The aim of the Act of Synod was to keep open a process of discernment about the rightness of the Church of England's decision to ordain women, to keep the highest possible degree of communion within each diocese, and to recognize and respect the integrity of different beliefs concerning the ordination of women. It could be said that this sort of continued working, repeated in many dioceses across the country, represents the spirit of the thinking contained in the House of Bishop's Manchester statement and in the theological document *In Communion*.

The main effect of the Act has been to set up a variety of working arrangements for those who cannot accept the episcopal ministry of those bishops who have been involved in the ordination of women. The following section displays snapshots of the way different dioceses have done this.

The Diocese of Southwark has a system of area bishops. Of a hundred parishes in the Woolwich area (of which Colin

Buchanan is bishop), seven have petitioned for 'extended episcopal oversight'. Such oversight is provided in the diocese by the Bishop of Fulham who is a suffragan Bishop of London, although, unlike the other suffragan bishops of that diocese, he has no distinct geographical area. His responsibilities are with those who oppose the ordination of women and he exercises these responsibilities not only in his own diocese, but also in the Diocese of Southwark and other neighbouring dioceses. This is then an example of the 'regional arrangements' made possible in the Act of Synod and in this capacity he serves about forty parishes. He also attends diocesan staff meetings in Southwark on a regular basis.

The Bishop of Fulham is involved in appointments to parishes that have previously petitioned for extended episcopal oversight. Appointments in the Church of England are made by the presentation of suitable candidates by the patron (who could be the Crown, the bishop or private individuals) to the parish and the bishop. Patronage is not, however, surrendered to the visiting bishop. Numbers are so small that it is hard to talk of established custom in the Instituting or Licensing of clergy, but Bishop Colin plans that this will be done by the area bishop with the visiting bishop present.

Bishop Colin aims to preach in all the parishes of his area. In preaching to congregations of those parishes who have opted for extended episcopal oversight, he says that people at times are surprised to understand the meaning of the decision that the PCC has taken.

Parish visitations are always undertaken by the archdeacons and the area bishop in the normal way, regardless of the request for pastoral oversight, as a visitation is not a sacramental or pastoral matter in the terms of the Act. The Act of Synod made it clear that diocesan bishops retained juridical responsibility for all the parishes in their dioceses. Continuing to engage in visitations and not surrendering patronage are examples of how that responsibility continues to be exercised.

The Diocese of Manchester has a similar area system. There are seventeen parishes in the diocese (out of 310) that have asked for extended episcopal oversight, and of these, seven are in the area served by the Bishop of Middleton. The Bishop of Beverley, one of the Provincial Episcopal Visitors, provides for the needs of these parishes. In many ways this results in a similar pattern to Woolwich. The Bishop of Beverley does not induct priests to these parishes as this is done by the diocesan bishops, but he is given a role to play by them. He is often asked to preach at the induction/licensing.

From then on the diocesan bishops may have little contact with the parishes unless particularly invited for a non-sacramental occasion. Some of the parishes do this, and others do not. Similarly, clergy from these parishes vary in their participation in the diocese or the deanery, and some play no part at all. Unsurprisingly this pattern is reflected by the laity. Both people and clergy from the seventeen parishes are always invited to diocesan and deanery events, but it is a matter of disappointment to diocesan staff that attendance is poor, even at events that do not involve a celebration of the eucharist or where the celebrant would be expected to be acceptable. For example, the Archbishop of York celebrated at the 150th anniversary of the diocese and even here attendance from these parishes was small.

The pastoral care offered by the Provincial Episcopal Visitors in Manchester is rated highly partly because PEVs are able to be present in the parishes they have been asked to serve on a more frequent basis than the diocesan bishops. They serve fewer parishes than diocesan bishops, and have little of the involvement in the running of a diocese and consequently clergy and congregations have the advantage of far more episcopal time being made available to them than the rest of the Church of England. The PEV also attends Manchester diocesan staff meetings on a regular basis and takes a full part in these alongside the Manchester area bishops.

When a parish that has opted for extended episcopal oversight becomes vacant, a diocesan bishop and the PEV will both attend a PCC meeting to discuss the needs of the parish. The PEV then becomes involved in the selection of the new priest, but this is problematic when more than one parish is involved. Manchester, like other dioceses, is having to cut its clergy numbers because of the lack of available priests and one way of doing this is to appoint one priest to serve two parishes. However, if one parish has asked for extended episcopal oversight and its neighbour has not, the finding of a priest who would be willing to serve both, and to respect the decision of both, is very difficult. Nonetheless the Diocese of Manchester is committed to fairness in the way that it cuts down its clergy posts and will not allow special pleading from a parish on the grounds of having opted for extended episcopal oversight. They do not solve the problem by appointing a priest solely to a parish when it would otherwise have had to share a priest with another parish. Some concerns have been expressed in other dioceses that there are attempts to misuse the Act in this way as there is emerging evidence that parishes have opted for extended episcopal oversight in the belief that this would prevent them from being part of a reorganization.

Clergy in the Diocese of Manchester who are opposed to the ordination of women have organized an informal chapter. Attendance is still expected at the deanery chapter, although this does not always happen. The group numbers about thirty, including retired priests. The group itself keeps contact with the diocesan bishop.

Overall, despite the above, it appears that female clergy are becoming well accepted, although it is harder in areas where there is a concentration of parishes opposed to women's ordination.

In Chester the picture is not widely different from the above. Chester is able to offer the services of an assistant bishop who is himself opposed to the ordination of women, as well as the services of the PEV. Of the seven petitioning parishes, most continue involvement with the diocese and those belonging to the informal Forward in Faith group mostly continue to be present at their deanery chapters. Accounts are given of the support offered to women clergy by those who are themselves opposed to the ordination of women.

In Sheffield, at the time of the vote, the diocesan and the suffragan bishops were opposed to the ordination of women and only two parishes had petitioned for extended episcopal oversight. In 1993 Bishop Michael Gear was appointed as Bishop of Doncaster, and since he was in favour of women priests, it meant that women could be ordained within the diocese.

The clergy opposed to the ordination of women were nevertheless encouraged by the diocesan to form an alternative chapter, the Hickleton chapter, even though attendance was still expected at the deanery chapters. From an early date a separate 'Chrism Mass' with re-affirmation of vows was also offered for members of this chapter and others. Although the diocesan was opposed to the ordination of women he was still willing for women to become incumbents, and indeed two women had responsibility for parishes prior to the ordination to priesthood, with sacramental cover from male colleagues. In many ways the women are integrated into the diocese, with sixteen of the twenty-five female clergy now in incumbent status posts. However, some events such as the forthcoming ordination of a male deacon in his own parish church, at a separate service from the other deacons, will probably not feel comfortable to the women priests or to others. Following the retirement of David Lunn (Bishop of Sheffield at the time of the vote), and the announcement of his successor there were further petitions and there are now twelve petitioning parishes in Sheffield (out of a total of 175). The new diocesan has visited them all and has invited the PEV to exercise extended episcopal oversight within the diocese. The Bishop of Doncaster is of the opinion that the matter was easier to deal with in Sheffield because when emotions were at their highest, immediately after the November 1992 vote, there was little problem in the diocese. Now that the issue has to be faced by those who were unhappy with the vote some of the heat has already gone out of the situation.

In some other dioceses alternative episcopal oversight is provided internally, i.e. by the first of the ways of working provided for in the Act of Synod. Before the Act of Synod was introduced the bishops in London had already devised the 'London Plan'. Using a rationale similar to the Act of Synod it provided episcopal care for those opposed to the ordination of women to the priesthood. More importantly, at that stage it provided for the ordination of women in a diocese, already divided into episcopal areas, where most of the bishops were not prepared to ordain women as priest or to license female priests. With the changes in diocesan and area episcopacy the plan has been changed. More of the bishops are prepared to ordain women to the priesthood and even more of them are prepared to license, including the diocesan. In the one area where the bishop will no longer do this, it can be done by one of the other area bishops. Episcopal oversight for the parishes who have requested alternative episcopal oversight comes from the Bishop of Fulham, mentioned above.

In Winchester an existing suffragan bishop, the Bishop of Basingstoke, provides alternative episcopal oversight. Apart from these special duties he operates within the diocese as any other suffragan would, including offering pastoral care to female priests. The clear difference with these approaches to fulfilling the requirements of the Act is that the bishop providing alternative episcopal oversight is clearly part of the diocesan structure and fulfilling other duties within the diocese. He does not focus on a single cause. The original intention of the Act (5.(3)) was that PEVs would work as suffragans in a diocese and spend only part of their time with the disaffected.

The provisions of the Act undoubtedly provide episcopal pastoral care for those who are opposed to the ordination of women, and for whom the diocesan bishop is no longer acceptable. It undoubtedly allows some who would otherwise have left the Church of England to stay within it. It preserves the diocesan system because the diocesan does not let go of his authority in a parish that has petitioned for extended episcopal oversight, and thus in some way preserves a degree of communion within the diocese.

It is regarded as less helpful by some of the evangelical parishes opposed to the ordination of women. The Act is tied to

a catholic view of priesthood where celebration of the sacraments is a key issue. For evangelicals the issue is headship, so
parishes could well be happy with a woman celebrant but not a
woman incumbent. There are some evangelical parishes that
have asked for the ministry of the PEVs. It is also possible that
the Act will be cited on a different issue by evangelicals. The
issue of the ordination of women is less important for many
than the possibility of ordaining practising gay persons. If the
church is seen to adopt a more liberal attitude on this, or if
individual bishops do the same, a few parishes are likely to vote
for alternative episcopal oversight because of this.

The provisions of the Act are only a very small part of
diocesan life, as many dioceses number those who have opted
for extended episcopal oversight in single figures. Numbers of
parishes who have taken resolutions A and B are also small. At
least in some cases it is for the sake of the few or 'because we
are not quite ready for a women yet'. There will be priests
outside of these parishes who are unhappy about the ordination
of women, and priests within some of them who do not share
the feelings of their congregation. A side effect of the Act can
occur when parishes find themselves in a team, or a united
benefice, with a parish that has opted for alternative episcopal
oversight. At the very least this reduces the scope of the main-
stream parish in its search for a new incumbent as women will
be unable to be considered. There is also a growing amount of
evidence that some men are put off from looking at a parish
because of resolutions A and B, let alone a church having
petitioned for alternative episcopal oversight.

The fear expressed by many is that extended episcopal oversight can lead to 'alternative episcopal care', what one bishop
described as 'a diocese within a diocese'. An unintended result
of the Act is that rather than promoting unity within the
diocese, opponents of the ordination of women can become
isolated from the rest of the diocese. We have seen this happening when parishes distance themselves from diocesan events and
clergy from involvement in the work of the diocese. It may be
argued that it is institutionalized in some dioceses by the provi-

sion of a separate 'Chrism Mass' in Holy Week, when clergy can renew their ordination vows to a bishop exercising extended episcopal oversight and celebrate without the presence of female priests. A similar provision is made in some dioceses at clergy conferences. Increasing isolation can lead to a hardening of the lines and an end to the sort of possibility of dialogue about change which Edwin Barnes, now one of the PEVs, called for in a speech about theological colleges in the debate upon the Act in 1993.

Fears are also expressed about the effects of having bishops who are associated with one particular viewpoint, and others who hold the same views, rather than being anchored in the day-to-day living of the church in a geographical area. The intention of the Act of Synod had been that PEVs would be working in a particular diocese as suffragans and then spend part of their time in their 'special' duties. Fears are expressed, however, that instead of that, they appear to spend much of their time working for the cause.

Other issues related to episcopal oversight are dealt with in ways consistent with the Act. Ordinations are a clear example of this. On the whole, ordinations of deacons are not considered to be an issue by the dioceses, although there is one such case cited above. There was no conscience clause in the Deacons' Measure, so grounds for the separate ordination of deacons are shaky. In some cases ordinations of priests are now done in a parish church where previously they would have been done centrally in the cathedral and occasionally the dissenting candidate(s) are ordained separately, by the bishop responsible for those opposed to the ordination of women. The ordination of a priest is by bishop and priests (both male and female), so some dioceses now ask the candidates to specify who will lay hands on them, where previously this was left open.

The Act provides that 'no person or body shall discriminate against candidates either for ordination or for appointment to senior office in the Church of England on the grounds of their views or positions about the ordination of women to the priesthood'. The Advisory Board of Ministry follows this line in making it clear, in its guidelines to selectors, that opposition to the ordination of women is not a barrier to ordination at bishop's selection conferences. This is consistent with the aim of the Act to maintain the 'highest degree of communion' within each diocese.

Regret has been expressed by some that there have not been more appointments of bishops opposed to the ordination of women. Under current procedures there is wide consultation in the appointment of diocesan and suffragan bishops, with a recognition of the conflict between having a number of established women priests and requests for a bishop opposed to the ordination of women. This makes it less likely that an opposing bishop will be appointed. It is worth mentioning, however, that of the three most senior bishops – of Canterbury, York and London – two are not in favour of women priests.

Sometimes the Act fails because its provisions are not properly adhered to and there are insufficient safeguards in the Act to make sure that this happens. Anecdotal evidence suggests that the wide consultation within the parish prescribed in the guidelines to the Act before the passing of a resolution does not always happen. Bishops report that congregations do not always understand the provisions that their PCC has made for them. In one suburban parish the PCC petitioned the diocesan bishop for episcopal duties in the parish to be carried out in accordance with the Act of Synod. A number of factors seem to have led to the passing of the resolution. The present wardens, who were members of the congregation at the time, estimate that three-quarters of the members of the congregation did not understand who the PEV was. They also report that there was no consultation with the congregation prior to the PCC vote. The present incumbent identifies a number of other features of the church which may have been relevant to the original decision. The church was heavily dependent upon its priest, who was strongly opposed to the ordination of women to the priesthood, and women were involved liturgically in only a limited way. At the same time the church had decreasing involvement with the wider church through diocesan or deanery events, increasing their isolation. During the time the petition was in force the regular practice in the intercessions during the Mass was to pray for the PEV and not for the diocesan. Following the appointment of the then incumbent to another parish the wardens sought advice outside the parish and re-established communication with the diocese. Following a visitation from the suffragan at which the congregation met together, there was then an overwhelming vote in the PCC to withdraw the petition (1997). Resolutions A and B remain in force in the parish, although the wardens estimate that only one member of the congregation would be unhappy with a woman as celebrant. Members of the congregation have since expressed the view that it was good to be back with Bishop N. again (the diocesan). There was a real sense in which they felt that they had been away from their diocese, reinforced by the refusal even to pray for the diocesan and the strong discouragement from keeping contact with the diocese.

These are not the only effects of the Act of Synod. To explore further one must look at the Act itself in relation to the original Measure by which the Church of England agreed to ordain women.

There seemed to be a striking change in thinking between the Measure and the Act of Synod. The Measure had clearly enunciated the intention of the Church of England that women, as well as men, should be ordained priest. The Act of Synod appeared to be a step back from that, giving space to the notion that there are two equally acceptable and opposing beliefs in the Church of England about the rightness of ordaining women. This is often expressed as the 'two integrities', taking its wording, to some extent, from the Act itself.

Effects that follow from this, or are at least affected by this way of thinking, push the church towards institutionalization of disunity and a polarization of positions. For those who oppose the ordination of women it gives some hope that the church will change, although many hold the view that this is a false hope. In late 1995 a bishop opposed to the ordination of women indicated to me that he did not regard the change as permanent and that women priests would die out. There is a striving among those opposed to the ordination of women, not to find ways of working within the Church of England as it is now, but to find more permanent ways of separation. Calls have been made in Synod for the PEVs to be allowed to sponsor candidates to Advisory Board of Ministry selection conferences, as if they were diocesan bishops. These candidates would be those who were identifying themselves as opposed to women priests, and at this stage unable or unwilling to act through the normal structures of the Church of England, the Diocesan Director of Ordinands and the diocesan bishop. This is always refused because the PEVs are suffragans, and not diocesans, and they would not, therefore, be able to place a candidate as they have no diocese of their own. It has led to calls for the PEVs to become full members of the House of Bishops, unlike other suffragans. Full membership of the House would then lead to membership of Synod, alongside diocesans. At the moment PEVs have to stand for election to Synod alongside the other suffragans. They have so far failed to be elected.

The belief that there are two equal and alternative views has led to the calls for a third 'traditionalist' Province within the Church of England. This was already evident within the Synod meeting that debated the Act of Synod, when a member from Lichfield asked the Chair of the House of Bishops whether the working party would 'give further consideration to the concept of a third province in view of the fact that it has support in the Church . . .'[1] Geoffrey Kirk, Secretary of Forward in Faith, continues to argue for a 'Free Province' through recent articles in *New Directions*, following the vote by Forward in Faith at its National Assembly in September 1997. Such a Province would consist of parishes which, by an agreed means, had opted into it. It would not therefore have the geographical boundaries that we would normally associate with a Province. The picture on a map would be rather like a mild case of chicken pox. The boundaries would also have to remain flexible as parishes would have to be able to opt in and out of the Province. The legal complications would be horrendous. It is argued that such a free Province would help to preserve the unity and diversity of the Church of England although one senses that the only real argument in its favour is 'to provide space and security for those who oppose women's ordination'.[2]

The Free Province issue highlights the issue of the relationship of the PEVs to Forward in Faith. Forward in Faith acts as an umbrella group to all organizations and individuals who are opposed to the ordination of women, although it probably deals only with a small number of such people as it is seen as separatist by many. It seeks to support those who are opposed to the ordination of women and to provide an ecclesial structure which will continue the orders of bishop and priest as the Church of England has hitherto received them (i.e. without women). In his article in *New Directions* in February 1998 Geoffrey Kirk makes it clear that the PEV system provides the basis on which to work for a Free Province. He writes of developing a distinctive pastoral and catechetical ethos among the parishes that have taken resolutions A, B, and C and of a National Pastoral Conference of clergy called to agree, among the PEV parishes, a policy on 'moral and doctrinal issues affecting us'. There is already a separate and parallel structure to the diocesan one existing in the Forward in Faith organization. Deans are appointed to areas of the country in a way that parallels the area or rural deans of the dioceses, although their areas are very much larger. There is other evidence for the building of an alternative structure to the diocesan one, for example Vocations Conferences have been run for those opposing women priests with the support of the PEVs and others. *New Directions* advertises special Post Ordination Training courses for the same constituency.

Forward in Faith is widely seen, not as protecting an existing constituency, but as promoting an increase. The clerical Chair of Southwark Forward in Faith writes in the Autumn 1997 Newsletter in the context of long-term plans to continue 'our faithful witness' and not just die off quietly: '. . . just listen to complaints from bishops (even our own) that our constituency is "campaigning" and that our orthodox bishops need their wings clipped! What are we supposed to do?' The full time Director of Forward in Faith (Stephen Parkinson) makes it clear in the July 1995 issue that the intention is to boost the numbers of priests opposing the ordination of women to the priesthood. The very existence of PEVs conveys the same message. If we appoint a bishop on the basis of one particular aspect of his ministry and it is that aspect that he is seen to work most within, then we must expect a certain attempt to pull others in the direction he has been appointed to defend. The question must then be asked, how far is this likely to promote unity?

On balance there is evidence that serious attempts have been made to make the Act work in practice, but the central aim of preserving unity and dialogue has suffered in the detail of those attempts. In particular the Act appears to have opened the way to increasing isolation of those opposed to the ordination of women, or at least of one particular group of those so opposed. Communion is thereby lessened.

Postscript

MONICA FURLONG

I suppose nothing is harder than for a large body to admit that it has made fundamental mistakes, though a surprising number of large bodies have made such admissions in recent years – South Africa, Russia, even the Roman Catholic Church (to some extent) in its attitude to Jews – and in each case they have been admired for their courage. It would be ridiculous to compare any suffering in the Church of England with the sufferings in South Africa, Russia or the Holocaust, and I would not dream of taking the comparison very far, except in so far that these examples remind us that major changes of attitude are possible, that once people begin to think differently things can move quite fast, and that far from being shameful an admission of error can be very healing.

Healing is needed urgently in the Church of England in the form of a change of attitudes to women – all women, but particularly women priests who are employed by the Church. It desperately needs to learn to value them and not permit any form of discrimination against them. The rest of society is far ahead of the Church in this respect, but within the Church there remains an astonishing lack of awareness, a complaisant certainty that women are conveniently disposable. The words used as the bishops defended the Act of Synod, and many, many words used in debates about women priests before and since the Measure was passed, indicate a lack of true awareness of the implication of what is being said and done. Ignorance, prejudice, and naivete are not the only problems. The double talk about two integrities, and all the fine words about compassion in the speeches supporting the Act, concealed an inability to face conflict and to acknowledge the simple fact that the Church of England cannot go in two directions at once – nobody can. A price was paid for that weakness, though not by the people who made the decision. And in a sense nothing was decided. A choice had, and still has, to be made, and it is a choice for reality.

Notes

Introduction

1. Margaret Webster, *A New Strength, A New Song*, Mowbray 1994.
2. *Uppity*, April 1993.
3. *Uppity*, December 1993.

1. Gender and the Act of Synod

My thanks to Lisa Forman Cody, Lois McNay, Christina Rees and Vincent Strudwick for their help in thinking through a number of the ideas in this chapter.

1. Hereafter referred to as the Measure.
2. For a fuller discussion of this, see Thomas Laqueur, *Making Sex. Body and Gender from the Greeks to Freud*, Harvard University Press 1990.
3. Episcopal Act of Synod 1993, Preamble (1) (a) (iii), p.1.
4. Episcopal Act of Synod 1993, Provincial Arrangements 5. (3) and (4), p.3.
5. See Laqueur, *Making Sex*.
6. Londa Schiebinger, *The Mind has No Sex? Women in the Origins of Modern Science*, Harvard University Press 1989, p.215.
7. See Cynthia Eagle Russet, *Sexual Science. The Victorian Construction of Womanhood*, Harvard University Press 1989.
8. For a discussion of these developments in the nineteenth century, particularly in relation to Christianity, see Leonore Davidoff and Catherine Hall, *Family Fortunes. Men and Women of the English Middle Class 1780–1850*, Hutchinson 1987.
9. Luce Irigaray, 'Sexual Difference' in her *An Ethics of Sexual Difference*, Cornell University Press 1993, p.5.
10. Mary Douglas, *Purity and Danger. An Analysis of the Concepts of Pollution and Taboo*, Routledge, revd edn 1996, p.3.
11. I am grateful to Vincent Strudwick for the use of his unpublished paper on the historical development of the episcopate. I have greatly

relied on his ideas for my argument here.

12. Response to audience questions after her talk, 'Dangerous Hands in Deep Waters. Some First Reflections on II Corinthians', King's College, London, 13 July 1998.

13. Henrietta Moore, *A Passion for Difference*, Polity Press 1994, p.27.

2. *A Theological Reflection – The Lost Anglican Tradition*

1. Cf. *Bonds of Peace*, a Statement by the House of Bishops of the Church of England, 1993, secs 4 and 5.

2. Cf. *The Priesthood of the Ordained Ministry*, a Report by the General Synod Board for Mission and Unity (GS 694), 1986, p.101.

3. *Bonds of Peace*, e.g., cites as an instance of communion the willingness of a bishop supporting the decision to ordain women as priests to invite an opponent bishop into his diocese to minister to opponent congregations. But in theological terms this is not 'communion' but courtesy and co-operation – truly desirable, but not the same thing.

4. For an authoritative summary of the main features of this tradition cf. *The Priesthood of the Ordained Ministry*, cited in n.2.

5. Cf. *Ordinatio Sacerdotalis*, an Apostolic Letter of Pope John Paul II, 1994, sec. 2; and *Inter Insigniores*, a Declaration of the Sacred Congregation for the Doctrine of the Faith, 1976, sec. 4.

6. These positions are at least close to ones condemned in the Decree *Lamentabili* of the Holy Office, 1907.

7. *The Priesthood of the Ordained Ministry* takes up a mediating position on this point: '. . . *the risen Christ*' (emphasis mine) 'has appointed and maintains a specially ordained ministry . . .' (p.99, para. 14). The Roman Catholic Church, in reply to ARCIC I, categorically reaffirms historical dominical institution: '. . . it was Christ himself who instituted the sacrament of Orders as the rite which confers the priesthood of the New Covenant' (*Response of the Holy See to the Final Report of the Anglican-Roman Catholic International Commission 1982*, The Incorporated Catholic Truth Society, London 1991, p.10).

8. If as St Luke affirms, one qualification for being recognized as an apostle was to have been a 'witness of his [Christ's] resurrection' (Acts 1.22), then clearly the supply of such persons would in time come to an end. St Paul likewise seems to base his own right to be called an 'apostle' on the fact that, however belatedly, he too had seen the risen Christ (I Cor. 15.8; cf. 9.1f.). The number and identity of those recognized as 'apostles' are indeterminate. cf. the varying lists of

names of 'the Twelve', and the possible apostolic status of Barnabas (Acts 14.14) and Andronicus and (?) Junias (Rom. 16.8).

9. *Catechism of the Catholic Church*, 1994, secs 1364–66.
10. Encyclical Letter of Pope Paul VI, *Mysterium Fidei*, 1965, sec. 38.
11. Discourse of Pope Pius XII at the International Congress on Pastoral Liturgy, Assisi 1956 (cited in J. Neuner and J. Dupuis (eds), *The Christian Faith*, Collins 1983, pp. 432f.).
12. *General Instruction on the Roman Missal of the Sacred Congregation for Divine Worship*, 1970 (cf. Neuner and Dupuis, op. cit., p.442).
13. Cf. *Priesthood of the Ordained Ministry*, paras 99–106.
14. ARCIC I, *The Final Report*, 'Ministry and Ordination', para. 13, CTS/SPCK 1982.
15. It is, of course, in order to avoid even a superficial outward resemblance of the wine to blood that in Catholic practice white wine is used for the sacrament.
16. Among bilateral discussions concerning the Anglican Communion may be mentioned, in addition to ARCIC, those with the Orthodox, Lutheran and Reformed Churches, and the negotiations between the Church of England and the Methodist Church. At the wider ecumenical level cf. the WCC Lima Text, *Baptism, Eucharist and Ministry*, and in England the Covenant negotiations which ended in failure in 1982.
17. Cf. *The Priesthood of the Ordained Ministry*, p.101: 'The disunity of the people of God imposes limitations on the exercise of the ordained ministry in the universal Church; but these do not remove its essentially universal character.'
18. We may be thankful that the Church in Wales realized this, and drafted its regulations for the ordination of women to the priesthood in 1997 accordingly.

3. One Lord, One Faith, One Baptism, but Two Integrities?

An earlier version of this chapter was given to the students and staff at Ripon College Cuddesdon (January 1997); the General Theological Seminary, New York (April 1997); the Oxford Diocesan Chapter of the Society of Catholic Priests (October 1997); the National Association of Diocesan Advisers in Women's Ministry (April 1998); and a study group of lay and ordained women in the Diocese of Worcester (April 1998). I am grateful to those present for their criticism and reflection.

1. Rowan Williams, 'Women and the Ministry: a case for theological

seriousness' in *Feminine in the Church* ed Monica Furlong, SPCK 1984, p.11.

2. In this chapter, the 1992 Measure, or simply the Measure, shall be taken to mean *The Ordination of Women to the Priesthood: Reference of Draft Legislation to the Diocesan Synods 1990*, Memorandum by the Standing Committee and Background Papers (GS Misc 336, 1990). On its passing by Parliament in November 1993 it became the Priests (Ordination of Women) Measure 1993. The 1993 Act of Synod, or simply the Act of Synod, or Act, shall be taken to mean *Ordination of Women to the Priesthood: Pastoral Arrangements*, a report by the House of Bishops which contains the documents *Bonds of Peace* and *Draft Episcopal Ministry Act of Synod 1993* (GS 1074). The Act was slightly amended and approved by the November 1993 session of General Synod as the Episcopal Ministry Act of Synod 1993: Important background thinking for the Act is to be found in the document *Being in Communion* (GS Misc 418, 1993).

3. GS Misc 336, 1990.

4. *Bonds of Peace*, para. 4.

5. *Bonds of Peace*, para. 5.

6. Although it has become focussed on the last few decades, readers should note that the debate about the ordination of women in the Church of England has a longer history. See Brian Heeney, *The Women's Movement in the Church of England 1850–1930*, OUP 1988 and especially Sheila Fletcher's superb biography of its greatest champion, *Maude Royden: a life*, Blackwells 1989.

7. Grace Sentamu, quoted by her father in General Synod, 5 July 1988 and cited by Margaret Webster, *A New Strength, A New Song*, Mowbray 1994, p.115.

8. *Bonds of Peace* is based largely on a slightly earlier document, *Being in Communion* (GS Misc 418,1993).

9. The Bishop of Richborough in *The Tablet*, 18 January 1997, p.75. It is worth noting that 'receptionism' describes far more accurately the eucharistic theology of Calvin, not Zwingli, the latter being better known for his 'memorialism'.

10. For a discussion and critique of recent historiography of the English Reformation see chapter 1 of Judith Maltby, *Prayer Book and People in Elizabethan and Early Stuart England*, CUP 1998. The late seventeenth-century Non-jurors do not make a happy precedent either; see Roger Turner, 'Bonds of Discord: alternative episcopal oversight examined in the light of Non-juring consecrations', *Ecclesiastical Law Journal* 3:17, 1995.

11. Rt Revd Stephen Sykes, *Report of the Proceedings of General Synod*,

November Group of Sessions 1993, p.986.

12. *The Tablet*, 18 January 1997, p.75.

13. Article 21 of the Thirty-Nine Articles.

14. The quotation is from a Donatist statement of their case made in 411. See Peter Brown, *Augustine of Hippo*, Faber 1967 and University of California Press, p.214. See also Robert F. Evans, *One and Holy: the Church in Latin Patristic Thought*, SPCK 1972, esp.pp.89–91.

15. *Issues in Human Sexuality* (GS Misc 382, 1991).

16. David Holloway, 'Wanting to Reform the Church', *Church Times*, 25 October 1996.

17. 'The Episcopal Ministry Act of Synod 1993: A theological and pastoral review' (The College of St George, Windsor Consultation, 20–22 April 1998). See also '"In the Light of Experience": a consultation to review the early years of the ordination of women in the Church of England' (The College of St George, Windsor Consultation, 22–24 September 1997), which provides a much more detailed and rigorous theological critique of the Act.

4. An Act of Betrayal

1. Archbishop of York in *Report of the Proceeding of General Synod*, 15 November 1984, p.1107.

2. *Report of the Proceedings of General Synod*, 8 July 1986, pp.632ff.

3. General Synod Draft Priests (Ordination of Women) Measure, Revision Committee Report (GS 830 Y), p.13.

4. Archbishop of York in *Report of the Proceedings of General Synod*, November Group of Sessions 1993, p.717.

5. Professor David McClean in *Report of the Proceedings of General Synod*, 8 July 1986, p.634.

6. Revd Martin Flatman in *Report of the Proceedings of General Synod*, November Group of Sessions 1993, p.723.

7. Revd Geoffrey Kirk, 'The Case for a Free Province', *Christian Challenge*, May 1998, p.8.

5. Working the Act

1. Peter Selby, *BeLonging: Challenge to a Tribal Church*, SPCK 1991, p.45.

2. In *The Times*, 11 October 1986.

3. 'The Elders of the Tribe', *BeLonging*, pp.56–64.

6. *What is Catholicity? A Methodist Looks at the Act*

1. Quoted in the *Methodist Recorder*, 2 July 1992.
2. Methodist Publishing House 1995.
3. Rowland Young, *Facts and Fancies*, William Tweedie 1880, p.12.
4. Frances Power Cobbe, *The Duties of Women*, London 1881, p.22.
5. Charles Gore, *The Mission of the Church*, London 1892, p.vii.
6. *Commitment to Mission and Unity*, Church House Publishing and Methodist Publishing House 1996, paras 45, 46.

7. *At the Grassroots: The Act in the Parishes*

1. *Report of the Proceedings of General Synod*, November Sessions 1993, p.801.
2. *New Directions*, February 1998, p.4.

Notes on Contributors

JOHN AUSTIN BAKER was born in 1928. Since ordination in 1954 he has worked as a parish priest, college and university lecturer, student chaplain, visiting professor, Canon of Westminster, Chaplain to the Speaker of the House of Commons and, till retirement, Bishop of Salisbury.

He served as a member and chairman of the Church of England Doctrine Commission, and on the Standing Committee of the WCC Faith and Order Commission. He chaired the Working Party which in 1982 published *The Church and the Bomb*, and was also for several years much involved in work for peace in Northern Ireland.

His own published works include *The Foolishness of God* (1970), *Travels in Oudamovia* (1976), *The Whole Family of God* (1981) and *The Faith of a Christian* (1996), as well as translations, and contributions to many symposia.

In 1991 he was awarded a Lambeth DD.

LESLEY BENTLEY is Vicar of St Philip, Westbrook, a large parish in the new town area of Warrington. She is Dean of Women's Ministry in the Diocese of Liverpool, and has been involved in this work for the last nine years. She is Chair of the Network of Diocesan Advisors in Women's Ministry, although views expressed in her contribution to this book are her own. Lesley began her ordained ministry in the Diocese of Derby where she was made Deaconess in 1982. She undertook two curacies, before being appointed to a curacy post with responsibility for the village of Cronton. She was appointed to Westbrook in 1995.

MONICA FURLONG is a writer and journalist, who has written a number of books on religious and spiritual issues, including *Merton*, a biography of Thomas Merton, and a biography of Thérèse of Lisieux. For nearly twenty years she has been particularly concerned with women's issues in the Church of England, and in particular, the issue of women's ordination. She was the Moderator of the Movement for the Ordination of Women from 1982–85, where she started a magazine *Chrysalis*, and was one of the founders of the St Hilda Community (started 1987), a group concerned with pioneering a new relationship between men and women in the church. She wrote a book, *A Dangerous Delight* (SPCK 1991) about women and power in the church. She opposed the Act of Synod. She attends Holy Trinity Church, Beckenham, where she serves on the PCC.

IAN JACKSON is a Methodist Circuit Minister. Born in Lancashire, he was educated in Manchester, Oxford and Birmingham where he trained for the ministry at Queen's College. He has worked in Walsall, a Liverpool housing estate, inner city Birmingham and south east London. He is married to Chrissy Ross. They have two daughters, Abigail and Miriam. They live and work in Greenwich engaging in ministry focussed on economic and social regeneration issues and the millennium. He has recently completed an MA at Kings, London where his thesis 'Subverting Virtue or Little by Little' explored the displacement of women from nineteenth-century religious life and the tactics they used to subvert the dominant culture. His particular concerns are to relate the church to civil society and to explore ways of being church which release human creativity and flair and enhance human freedom and compassion.

JUDITH MALTBY is Chaplain and Fellow of Corpus Christi College, Oxford. A cradle Anglican raised in the 'Biretta Belt' of the American Episcopal Church, she has lived in England since 1979. She did her doctoral studies at Cambridge where she held a Research Fellowship at Newnham College and has published on the political and religious history of sixteenth- and seventeenth-century England with the Royal Historical Society and Cambridge University Press, including *Prayer Book and People in Elizabethan and Early Stuart England* (CUP 1998). She taught in theological education for seven years (both Methodist and Anglican) before coming to Oxford, and while on the staff of Salisbury and Wells, assisted in a local parish. She was an active member of the Movement for the Ordination of Women, and is a current member of Women and the Church (WATCH), the Society of Catholic Priests, the Further Degrees Panel of the Advisory Board of Ministry and a member of the Formal Conversations between the Methodist Church and the Church of England.

JEAN MAYLAND was born in 1936 and educated at the Orme Girls' School, Newcastle under Lyme and Lady Margaret Hall, Oxford. In 1959 she married Ralph, an Anglican priest who later became Canon Treasurer of York Minster. They have two daughters and three granddaughters.

She taught history and religious education in a number of schools and then taught at High Melton College of Education. For ten years she lectured in Old Testament and Liturgy on the Northern Ordination

Course. She is now Associate Secretary for the Community of Women and Men in the Church at the Council of Churches for Britain and Ireland.

She was a Member of Church Assembly and General Synod from 1965 to 1990. She served from 1975 to 1991 on the Central Committee of the World Council of Churches. For ten years she was a member of the Study Committee of the Conference of European Churches and served as Moderator for five of those ending at the Graz Assembly in 1997.

She was a founding member of the Movement for the Ordination of Women (MOW) and now serves on the Committee of Women and the Church (WATCH).

She was ordained deacon in 1991 and priest in 1994.

PETER SELBY is currently the Bishop of Worcester. From 1992 to 1997 he held the William Leech Professorial Fellowship in Applied Christian Theology at Durham University, after having served as Area Bishop of Kingston from 1984 to 1992. His main theological interest at the moment is in the encounter between faith and economics, about which he wrote in his most recent book, *Grace and Mortgage: the language of faith and the debt of the world* (Darton, Longman and Todd 1997), which takes Dietrich Bonhoeffer's prison reflections as its starting point. He was convenor of the 1998 Lambeth Conference's subsection on international debt.

JANE SHAW is Dean, and Fellow and Tutor in History, at Regent's Park College, Oxford. She teaches History, Theology and Women's Studies in the university. She is a priest in the Church of England, and serves as Non-Stipendiary Minister at the University Church of St Mary the Virgin, Oxford. She lived for eight years in the USA, where she was active in the Episcopal Church. She has a Ph.D in History from the University of California at Berkeley, and a Master's degree in Divinity from Harvard University. She has published articles on feminist theory and theology, and on seventeenth- and eighteenth-century cultural and religious history, is co-editor of *Culture and the Nonconformist Tradition* (University of Wales Press) and is currently writing a book about miracles in Enlightenment England.

Priests (Ordination of Women) Measure 1993
Code of Practice

(Issued by the authority of the House of Bishops, January 1994)

Introduction

1. By the enactment of the Priests (Ordination of Women) Measure 1993, and its associated Canons, the Church of England has opened the order of priests to women. This entails that the order is a single whole and that women duly ordained priests share equally with their male counterparts in the exercise of its ministry, in synodical government and in consideration for suitable appointments.

2. The House of Bishops and the General Synod have recognised that there have been and will continue to be deeply held differences of conviction about the ordination of women to the priesthood and that some, bishops, clergy and lay people, find it unacceptable. Christian charity and the exercise of true pastoral care require that careful provision be made to respect as far as possible their position while doing as little as possible to prejudice the full exercise of priestly ministry by women.

3. The Measure contains provisions designed to protect the position of individuals and parishes. These have been supplemented by the pastoral arrangements embodied in the Episcopal Ministry Act of Synod 1993.[1] It is important that these provisions of the Measure and the Act of Synod are fully honoured. Some other matters are not easily or appropriately provided for in legislation, but are dealt with in this Code of Practice. This Code, therefore, explains and complements but in no way qualifies or detracts from the legislation.

Declarations by Diocesan Bishops

4. Section 2 of the Measure provides that a diocesan bishop in office at the relevant date may make one or more of the following declarations:

---

[1] The thinking behind the Act of Synod was set out in the statements issued by the House of Bishops in January and June 1993 (the latter under the title 'Bonds of Peace') and in the associated theological paper 'Being in Communion' (GS Misc 418).

(a) that a woman is not to be ordained within the diocese to the office of priest; or

(b) that a woman is not to be instituted or licensed to the office of incumbent or priest-in-charge of a benefice, or of team vicar for a benefice, within the diocese; or

(c) that a woman is not to be given a licence or permission to officiate as a priest within the diocese

It is a matter for each diocesan bishop in office at the date on which the Canon comes into force to decide whether or not to make any or all of these declarations. Because of the effect of the declarations on his suffragans, and on the diocese as a whole, it will be appropriate for the bishop to consult with other bishops in the diocese and with the Bishop's Council. It will, however, be recognised that the object of Section 2 is to protect the position of the diocesan bishop and the decision is his alone.

5. The measure provides that a suffragan bishop shall act in accordance with a declaration made by the diocesan bishop. Diocesan bishops who elect not to make any or all of the declarations provided will fully respect the views of suffragan, area and assistant bishops, as the case may be, in the diocese and will not expect or require any bishop to act against his conscience.

6. Each diocesan bishop will inform any area, suffragan or assistant bishop in the diocese, and the Bishop's Council, as to whether he has made any, or all, of the declarations provided in Section 2 of the Measure.

7. There may be diocesan bishops who, whilst not wishing themselves to ordain women to the priesthood, would not wish to inhibit such ordinations taking place in their diocese. In such cases the diocesan bishop would not make the declaration provided in Section 2(1)(a) but would either arrange for another bishop to ordain women to the priesthood in the diocese or allow the Archbishop or his Commissary to do so in accordance with the provisions of Section 11 of the Episcopal Ministry Act of Synod 1993. The diocesan bishop would retain, however, his role as Ordinary and provide, either directly or through his suffragans, continuing pastoral oversight and care to any woman so ordained or admitted to office.

Lay Women or Women Deacons Seeking Ordination to the Priesthood

8. In line with the arrangements envisaged above, a lay woman or a woman deacon wishing her vocation to the priesthood to be tested should, in any diocese where declarations under Section 2 of the Measure are not in force, apply in the usual way to her diocesan bishop, who will then arrange for her application to be considered in whatever way is appropriate in the circumstances of his diocese.

9. In any diocese where the bishop has declared that a woman is not to be ordained to the office of priest, a lay woman or a woman deacon wishing her vocation to the priesthood to be tested should approach the bishop of a neighbouring diocese, normally that nearest her place of residence. In the case of a woman deacon, she must first inform her own bishop of her intention to do this.

10. The bishop to whom application is made, if prepared to pursue that application, shall inform the bishop of the candidate's own diocese that application has been made to him and invite the bishop to let him have any observations on the candidate. When the bishop to whom application is made has decided whether or not the candidate is to be sponsored to a bishop's selection conference, he shall inform the other bishop accordingly. If accepted for training, the candidate will be sponsored by the bishop to whom the application was made, who will accept the same financial responsibility for training as for that of all other candidates he sponsors.

11. Where the application is in respect of Non-Stipendiary Ministry, a sponsoring bishop is required to undertake to find an appropriate placement. A neighbouring bishop approached by a woman candidate for NSM Ministry under this Code of Practice will have to consider the possibility of the candidate receiving a licence, which may depend upon her ability to move to his diocese.

12. The House of Bishops has agreed guidelines for the testing and discernment of vocation and the preparation for ordination to the priesthood of women already in deacon's orders when the Measure comes into force.

Ordination Services

13. The conduct of ordination services, whether held in a cathedral or a parish church, is a matter for the diocesan bishop. He determines who will ordain, and with the ordaining bishop decides, after due consultation, where and when individuals are ordained, and which priests should be present and take part in the laying on of hands.

14. In the case of ordinations to the diaconate, it would be inappropriate to exclude candidates of one sex from a particular ordination service, or to arrange a separate service for ordinands opposed to the ordination of women to the priesthood. As regards ordinations to the priesthood, bishops will wish to show the appropriate sensitivity. For example, where a male deacon is serving in a parish which has passed Resolution A, the practice in a number of dioceses of holding ordinations to the priesthood in the parish church of the parish in which a candidate is serving as a deacon might be found especially helpful. It would be inappropriate to hold an ordination at which a woman deacon was to be ordained priest in the parish church of a parish which has passed Resolution A.

15. Bishops commonly welcome the sharing in the laying on of hands by

priests related to, or well-known to, individual candidates. Where an ordination takes place in a diocese where the bishop has made a declaration reflecting his continuing opposition to the ordination of women or in a parish where Resolution A is in force, the ordaining bishop would not invite a woman priest to take part in this way.

Resolutions by Parochial Church Councils under the Measure

16. Under Section 3 of the Measure it is open to parochial church councils (PCCs) to pass either or both of the resolutions in Schedule 1 to the Measure, viz.:
    A. That this PCC would not accept a woman as the minister who presides at or celebrates the Holy Communion or pronounces the Absolution in the parish;
    B. That this PCC would not accept a woman as the incumbent or priest-in-charge of the benefice or as a team vicar of the benefice.

Petition by Parochial Church Councils under the Act of Synod

17. Under Section 7 of the Episcopal Ministry Act of Synod the Parochial Church Council of a parish where Resolution A or B is in force may petition the diocesan bishop concerned to the effect that appropriate episcopal duties in the parish should be carried out in accordance with the diocesan, regional or provincial arrangements described in the Act. (This provision does not apply to a parish in which there is a parish church cathedral.) Once he has received such a petition, the diocesan bishop will consult the minister and the Parochial Church Council in accordance with Section 8 of the Act, and consider the petition bearing in mind the provisions of Section 10.

18. Before considering whether to petition the diocesan bishop, a PCC will need to consult widely within the parish. The advice of the appropriate Provincial Episcopal Visitor may be sought in connection with the making or consideration of any such petition. Views on the desirability of making a petition may differ widely and the Council will need to be sensitive to the difficulties which may arise for individuals. Deaneries should make plans which will allow for those with different opinions to be accommodated in other parishes. Consideration will need to be given to the position of NSMs, LNSM, Readers and other ministers as well as of the laity.

19. A petition may be withdrawn by the Parochial Church Council at any time, subject to the same procedures as applied in passing the petition. In any case, any arrangements made as a result of a petition must be reviewed at least once every five years (Section 9 of the Act).

Exercise of Priestly Ministry in a Parish

20. Bishops will expect full and sensitive observance of the rights given to PCCs under the Measure and already enjoyed by incumbents under

Canon Law. In particular, they will seek to ensure that rural deans and others arranging services in a parish will make no arrangements which would contravene a PCC resolution or override the wishes of the incumbent.

21. In circumstances where the incumbent is ill or incapacitated the arrangements made for priestly ministry will be consonant with the incumbent's own past practice.

22. During a vacancy in a benefice the practice which obtained prior to that vacancy will be continued, unless a resolution to the contrary is passed by the PCC under the provisions of Section 3 of the Measure.

23. The House of Bishops would regard it as an abuse of Section 2(7) of the Measure, and of Canon C8, for an incumbent to use those powers to further a policy of a regular ministry of women priests in the parish(es) of his benefice.

Occasional Offices

24. The Measure enables a PCC to carry Resolution A declining to accept a woman as the minister who presides at or celebrates the Holy Communion in the parish. Where the Holy Communion is combined with a Marriage or Funeral Service, if Resolution A is in force in a parish, a woman priest would not be able to act as president. Where Resolution A is *not* in force the House will expect incumbents to respect the wishes of those concerned as to the gender of the president.

Extra-Parochial Ministry

25. Before licensing a priest to a college, hospital, prison or other institution under the Extra-Parochial Ministry Measure 1967, a bishop consults with the appropriate authorities of the institution. These consultations will cover the question of the acceptability of a woman priest where such an appointment is contemplated. The Hospital Chaplaincies Council has produced guidance on arrangements in hospitals following the implementation of the Priests (Ordination of Women) Measure.

Appointments and Ministry in Multi-Parish Benefices, Team Ministries, etc.

26. The body which makes the decision to pass Resolution A or B is the Parochial Church Council of a parish (or of a conventional district). A parish may, however, either be part of a larger unit comprising a single benefice, or contain within itself several churches, perhaps of differing traditions, which may or may not have formal District Church Councils. In these situations, and in some related cases such as Group Ministries, especial sensitivity will be required in making appointments.

27. The legislation provides that where a benefice comprises more than one parish, the passing of Resolution B by any one PCC prevents the appointment of a woman as incumbent of the benefice. This position must be respected by all concerned, but each PCC within such a benefice should recognise the effect and implications which carrying Resolution B will have for the benefice as a whole.

28. Resolution A applies only to an individual parish, and not to other parishes in the same benefice. Its existence will, however, limit the scope of the ministry of any woman priest serving within the benefice. The fact that one of the parishes had carried Resolution A would need to be carefully weighed before a woman priest was appointed.

29. Similar considerations apply in the case in which a parish contains churches of different traditions. Where a District Church Council exists it may express a view on the matters covered by Resolutions A and B (though that expression of view would have no formal legal effect). Where there is no District Church Council, the bishop may ask the incumbent and churchwardens to ascertain the balance of opinion within the congregation. It would be inappropriate to seek to appoint a woman as incumbent of a parish which contained a church whose congregation found her ministry unacceptable. The same would be true of the appointment of a woman team vicar or assistant curate whose area of responsibility would include that church; in other cases, where there were to be limitations on the area in which she was to exercise her ministry, an appointment of a woman to serve in the parish could still be appropriate.

Diocesan, Archdeaconry and Deanery Services

30. Even where a resolution under Section 4(a) of the Measure is not in force for the cathedral, bishops will seek themselves, and will encourage others, to be sensitive in making arrangements for diocesan, archdeaconry and deanery services in circumstances where women priests serve in the area but there are also a significant number who find the exercise of priestly functions by a woman unacceptable. Where this latter position is known to be predominant it would be inappropriate for a woman priest to exercise those priestly functions; in other cases, the identity of the officiant should be made known in advance. If such practice is adopted, it should be followed whether the officiant at a particular service is female or male. Subject to that, when the clergy of an area, or the holders of particular offices such as that of rural dean or canon, are invited to robe, the invitation will apply in all cases without discrimination as to gender. Similarly there should be no discrimination in regard to participation in chapter and other official meetings on the grounds of gender or attitude to women's priestly ordination.

Care of Those who Resign from Office

31. The House of Bishops has affirmed that its members will continue to be concerned for the pastoral care of, and the practical provision for, those clergy who make the declaration provided in the Schedule to the Ordination of Women (Financial Provisions) Measure 1993 and their families. The House hopes that any deacon or priest who may be considering making that declaration, or who has concluded, in conscience, that he or she must do so, will continue to be in touch with the diocesan bishop of the diocese in which he or she chooses to reside.

Conclusion

32. The arrangements in the Priests (Ordination of Women) Measure and the Episcopal Ministry Act of Synod provide a framework within which those members of the Church of England of differing views on the ordination of women to the priesthood can seek to remain in the highest possible degree of communion with one another. Mutual respect and trust will be essential if the arrangements are to work successfully. The aim must be for all to continue to participate in every aspect of the Church's life to the fullest extent which individual conscience will allow, showing at all times that charity, courtesy, and respect for others which are among the hallmarks of the true Christian.

Church House, SW1   On behalf of the House of Bishops
12 January 1994   George Cantuar:
                                                                                      Chairman

General Synod
Episcopal Ministry
Act of Synod 1993

(As approved at the November 1993 Group of Sessions)

Passed by the General Synod to make provision for the continuing diversity of opinion in the Church of England as to the ordination and ministry of women as priests, and for related matters.

Whereas:

(1) The Church of England through its synodical processes has given final approval to a Measure to make provision by Canon for enabling women to be ordained to the priesthood;

(2) The bishop of each diocese continues as the ordinary of his diocese;

(3) The General Synod regards it as desirable that –

   (a) all concerned should endeavour to ensure that –

      (i) discernment in the wider Church of the rightness or otherwise of the Church of England's decision to ordain women to the priesthood should be as open a process as possible;

      (ii) the highest possible degree of communion should be maintained within each diocese; and

      (iii) the integrity of differing beliefs and positions concerning the ordination of women to the priesthood should be mutually recognised and respected;

   (b) the practical pastoral arrangements contained in this Act of Synod should have effect in each diocese.

Now it is hereby declared as follows:

Ordinations and Appointments

1. Except as provided by the Measure and this Act no person or body shall discriminate against candidates either for ordination or for appointment to senior office in the Church of England on the grounds of their views or positions about the ordination of women to the priesthood.

Appropriate Arrangements

2. Three types of arrangements may be made in order to provide an
   appropriate ministry for those who are opposed, namely –
   (a) diocesan arrangements to be made by the diocesan bishop in
       accordance with section 3 below;
   (b) regional arrangements to be made by the diocesan bishops of each
       region in accordance with section 4 below;
   (c) provincial arrangements to be made by the archbishops of the
       province in accordance with section 5 below.

Diocesan Arrangements

3. The diocesan bishop shall make arrangements so far as possible
   within his own diocese for appropriate care and oversight of the
   clergy and parishes in the diocese.

Regional Arrangements

4. (1) Whenever possible the diocesan bishops of each region acting
       jointly shall from time to time nominate from within their region
       for the purpose of this Act of Synod one or more bishops who are
       opposed.
   (2) Each bishop so nominated shall, in addition to his other duties, be
       approved by the archbishop of the province to carry out for any
       parish in the region such episcopal duties as the diocesan bishop
       concerned may request.
   (3) In subsection (1) above, except where the context otherwise
       requires, 'bishop' means a diocesan bishop, suffragan bishop or a
       full-time stipendiary assistant bishop serving in the region in
       question.

Provincial Arrangements

5. (1) The Archbishop of Canterbury shall from time to time take steps
       to secure the appointment of up to two additional suffragan
       bishops for his diocese to act as provincial episcopal visitors for
       the purposes of this Act of Synod in the province of Canterbury.
   (2) The Archbishop of York shall from time to time take steps to
       secure the appointment of one additional suffragan bishop for his
       diocese to act as a provincial episcopal visitor for the purposes of
       this Act of Synod in the province of York.
   (3) Each provincial episcopal visitor shall be commissioned by the
       archbishop of the province to carry out, or cause to be carried
       out, for any parish in the province such episcopal duties, in
       addition to his other duties, as the diocesan bishop concerned
       may request. The provincial episcopal visitor shall work with the
       diocesan bishop concerned in enabling extended pastoral care and
       sacramental ministry to be provided.

(4) Each provincial episcopal visitor shall act as spokesman and adviser for those who are opposed and shall assist the archbishops in monitoring the operation of the Act of Synod.

6. Where a vacancy occurs in the office of provincial episcopal visitor, the archbishop of the province concerned shall, before taking the steps referred to in section 5 above to secure the appointment of an additional suffragan bishop, consult the other provincial episcopal visitor or visitors and all other bishops who are directly concerned.

Parochial Church Council Petition

7. (1) Subject to subsection (2) below where a resolution set out in Schedule 1 to the Measure is in force, a decision may be taken by the parochial church council of the parish concerned to petition the diocesan bishop concerned to the effect that appropriate episcopal duties in the parish should be carried out in accordance with this Act of Synod.

  (2) Subsection (1) shall not apply in relation to a parish in which there is a parish church cathedral.

8. (1) Subject to section 10 below, on receiving any such petition the diocesan bishop shall, either personally or through his representative, consult with the minister and the parochial church council of the parish concerned; and having done so he shall make appropriate arrangements for episcopal duties to be carried out in the parish in accordance with this Act of Synod.

  (2) Where any such arrangements are made or proposed, the minister and the parochial church council of the parish concerned may seek the advice of the provincial episcopal visitor in connection with the matter.

9. (1) Where a parochial church council has presented a petition in accordance with section 7 above, the council may at any time take a further decision for the withdrawal of the petition; and, subject to section 10 below, upon the withdrawal of the petition the diocesan bishop concerned shall ensure that any arrangements made in pursuance thereof are cancelled.

  (2) Where a parochial church council has presented such a petition, the council shall review the working of any arrangements in force in pursuance thereof at least once in every period of five years.

10. Where a parochial church council has presented or withdrawn a petition in accordance with section 7 or 9 above and the diocesan bishop concerned is not satisfied that –

  (a) except where notice of a vacancy has been sent to the secretary of the council under section 7(4) of the Patronage (Benefices) Measure 1986, the secretary of the council gave to the members of the council at least four week's notice of the time and place of the meeting at which the motion proposing the resolution in question was to be considered;

(b) the meeting was attended by at least one half of the members of the council entitled to attend;

(c) at least two thirds of the members of the council present and voting were in favour of the resolution in question; and

(d) the minister was in favour of the resolution in question, whether or not he was present and voted,

he shall not be obliged to make arrangements of the kind mentioned in section 8 above or to cancel any such arrangements, but he may do so if he thinks fit.

Ordination etc. by Archbishop or his Commissary

11. (1) Subject to subsections (2) and (3) below, where the bishop of a diocese has indicated that he is opposed and, in the case of a bishop in office at the relevant date, that he is unwilling to make a declaration under section 2 of the Measure, the ordination to the priesthood of women from the diocese and their licensing and institution shall be carried out by the archbishop concerned, either personally or through a bishop acting as commissary; and the archbishop shall cause the archiepiscopal seal to be affixed to any documents that are needed for that purpose.

(2) The archbishop shall act under subsection (1) above either at the request of the diocesan bishop concerned or in pursuance of his metropolitical jurisdiction, but shall not so act unless he is satisfied that the diocesan bishop concerned has no objection.

(3) Subsection (1) above shall not apply where the bishop of a diocese has made arrangements for the ordination of women to the priesthood and their licensing and institution to be carried out by another bishop.

Interpretation

12. (1) In this Act of Synod –

'the Measure' means the Priests (Ordination of Women) Measure 1993;

'minister' has the same meaning as in the Care of Churches and Ecclesiastical Jurisdiction Measure 1991;

'opposed' means opposed to the promulgation of the relevant Canon;

'parish church cathedral' has the same meaning as in Part II of the Measure;

'provincial episcopal visitor' means a suffragan bishop appointed as such in pursuance of section 5 above;

'region' means an area, comprising two or more dioceses in a province, which is designated by the archbishop of the province as a region for the purposes of this Act of Synod;

'relevant Canon' means the Canon of the Church of England

enabling a woman to be ordained to the office of priest;

'relevant date' means the date on which the relevant Canon is promulged;

'senior office' means any of the following offices, that is to say, archbishop, diocesan bishop, suffragan bishop, dean or provost of a cathedral church, archdeacon and residentiary canon in a cathedral church.

(2) This Act of Synod shall apply in relation to a guild church designated and established under section 4 of the City of London (Guild Churches) Act 1952 as it applies in relation to a parish, but as if the references to the parochial church council of the parish were references to the guild church council of the guild church and the references to the minister were references to the vicar of the guild church.

(3) Any arrangements made under sections 2 to 5 above and any action taken under section 11 above by an archbishop in connection with the ordination of women to the priesthood, shall be without prejudice to the jurisdiction of the diocesan bishop concerned.

Citation and commencement

13. This Act of Synod may be cited as the Episcopal Ministry Act of Synod 1993 and shall come into force on the coming into force of the Measure.